The Routledge Guidebook to Einstein's *Relativity*

Albert Einstein, one of the most prolific scientists of the twentieth century, developed the theory of relativity which was crucial for the advancement of modern physics. Young Einstein identified a paradox between Newtonian Mechanics and Maxwell's equations which pointed to a flawed understanding of space and time by the scientists of the day. In *Relativity*, Einstein presents his findings using a minimal amount of mathematical language, but the text can still be challenging for readers who lack an extensive scientific background.

The Routledge Guidebook to Einstein's Relativity expands on and supplements this seminal text, by exploring:

- the historical context of Einstein's work and the background to his breakthroughs
- details of experimental verification of special and general relativity
- the enduring legacy of Einstein's theories and their implications for future scientific breakthroughs.

This is an essential introduction for students of physics, philosophy and history in understanding the key elements of the work and the importance of this classic text to society today.

James Trefil is Robinson Professor of Physics at George Mason University, USA. In 2000 he received the Andrew W. Gemant Award from the American Institute of Physics for outstanding and sustained contributions in bridging the gap between science and society.

THE ROUTLEDGE GUIDES TO THE GREAT BOOKS

Series Editor Anthony Gottlieb

The Routledge Guides to the Great Books provide ideal introductions to the work of the most brilliant thinkers of all time, from Aristotle to Marx and Newton to Wollstonecraft. At the core of each Guidebook is a detailed examination of the central ideas and arguments expounded in the great book. This is bookended by an opening discussion of the context within which the work was written and a closing look at the lasting significance of the text. *The Routledge Guides to the Great Books* therefore provide students everywhere with complete introductions to the most important, influential and innovative books of all time.

Available:

Forthcoming:

Routledge Guides to the Great Books

The Routledge Guidebook to Einstein's *Relativity*

James
Trefil

 Routledge
Taylor & Francis Group

LONDON AND NEW YORK

First published in The Routledge Guides to the Great Books series in 2015
by Routledge
2 Park Square, Milton Park, Abingdon, Oxon OX14 4RN

and by Routledge
711 Third Avenue, New York, NY 10017

Routledge is an imprint of the Taylor & Francis Group, an informa business

British Library Cataloguing in Publication Data
A catalogue record for this book is available from the British Library

Library of Congress Cataloging in Publication Data
Trefil, James, 1938– author.
The Routledge guidebook to Einstein's Relativity / James Trefil.
   pages cm. – (Routledge guides to the great books)
   Includes bibliographical references and index.
   1. Einstein, Albert, 1879–1955. Grundlage der allgemeinen
   Relativitätstheorie. 2. Einstein, Albert, 1879–1955. Über die spezielle und
   die allgemeine Relativitätstheorie. 3. General relativity (Physics)
   4. Special relativity (Physics) I. Title.
   QC173.6.T735 2015
   530.11–dc23   2014030949

ISBN: 978-0-415-72345-9 (hbk)
ISBN: 978-0-415-72346-6 (pbk)
ISBN: 978-1-315-73077-6 (ebk)

Typeset in Aldus
by HWA Text and Data Management, London

This book is dedicated to my grandchildren,
Sofia, Nellie, Maria and Jack

CONTENTS

SERIES EDITOR'S PREFACE

"The past is a foreign country," wrote the British novelist, L. P. Hartley, "they do things differently there." The greatest books in the canon of the humanities and sciences can be foreign territory, too. This series is a set of excursions written by expert guides who know how to make such places become more familiar.

All the books covered in this series, however long ago they were written, have much to say to us now, or help to explain the ways in which we have come to think about the world. Each volume is designed not only to describe a set of ideas, and how they developed, but also to evaluate them. This requires what one might call a bifocal approach. To engage fully with an author, one has to pretend that he or she is speaking to us; but to understand a text's meaning, it is often necessary to remember its original audience, too. It is all too easy to mistake the intentions of an old argument by treating it as a contemporary one.

The *Routledge Guides to the Great Books* are aimed at students in the broadest sense, not only those engaged in formal study. The intended audience of the series is all those who want to understand the books that have had the largest effects.

Anthony Gottlieb
Series editor Anthony Gottlieb is the author of *The Dream of Reason: A History of Philosophy from the Greeks to the Renaissance*

AUTHOR'S PREFACE

No scientist is better known to the general public than Albert Einstein. The image of the kindly grandfather with frizzy hair is firmly embedded in our consciousness, and it was no surprise that he was named 'Man of the Century' by *Time Magazine*.

Yet when it comes to understand what Einstein actually did, the situation is very different. The Theory of Relativity remains something of a mystery to those who haven't learned about it in a formal physics course, and this mystery probably explains some of the aura that surrounds him in the public mind. Einstein himself devoted considerable effort to remedying this situation, and his book *Relativity* (1916) is one of several attempts he made to explain his work at the popular level. Given that relativity was the first great scientific revolution of the twentieth century (followed later by quantum mechanics), the idea that relativity should be understood by the culturally literate citizen makes a lot of sense.

The book you are about to read is meant to be a companion to Einstein's work. It is, in the old-fashioned sense, a commentary on *Relativity* and not a stand-alone volume. There are many reasons why such a companion is needed. For one thing, since Einstein wrote his book, great strides have been made in experimental physics. This means that tests of both the special and general theories have been carried out at levels of precision that Einstein could not have imagined. Indeed, with the widespread availability of the global positioning system, relativity can be said to have moved from the realm of abstract theory to the realm of nuts and bolts engineering. Exploring the effect that these developments have had on the theory of relativity will be one of the main themes of this book.

In addition, since Einstein's time enormous progress has been made in our understanding of the fundamental forces of nature. In essence, while general relativity remains our best theory of gravity, it gives a picture of gravity that is different from our picture of other forces. Bringing gravity and the other forces of nature into harmony remains a major problem (some would say *the* major problem) in theoretical physics—a problem that was just beginning to be appreciated in Einstein's time. We will explore this problem in some detail in the final chapters of this book.

Einstein's book is written in short chapters—often only a few pages long. In the commentary, Einstein's chapters are grouped together, and each chapter in the commentary begins with a statement giving the chapters in *Relativity* that deal with the subject matter in question. This is followed by a short summary of the themes of Einstein's exposition, followed in turn by the development of the ideas needed to support Einstein's arguments.

As with any book, I received valuable input from colleagues with whom I shared drafts of the manuscript. With the usual caveat that any errors that remain are my responsibility alone, I would like to thank my wife, Wanda O'Brien-Trefil, Jeff Newmeyer, and Janina Blonski for their help.

James Trefil
Fairfax, Virginia

1

EINSTEIN'S LIFE

If my theory of relativity is proven successful, Germany will claim me as a German and France will declare that I am a citizen of the world. Should my theory prove untrue, France will say that I am a German and Germany will declare that I am a Jew.

Albert Einstein, 1922

If the dismissal of Jewish scientists means the annihilation of contemporary German science, then we shall do without science for a few years!

Adolf Hitler to Max Planck, 1933

Albert Einstein was born on March 15, 1879 in the town of Ulm, and no, he didn't flunk high school math. The town is now part of Germany, but had only joined the newly created German empire in 1871, having been part of the Kingdom of Württemburg before that. His parents, Hermann and Pauline, were what would be called today members of the upper middle class. His father was involved in manufacturing, a partner in a firm that produced feather beds at the time of Albert's birth.

The family were assimilated Jews, as is evidenced by the fact that they did not give their son a biblical name. Thus, Albert grew up in a liberal atmosphere as far as religion was concerned (although he did go through an adolescent period of hyper-religiosity). He apparently had a happy childhood. His father, an easy-going man, frequently read to the family and his mother was an accomplished pianist. In addition, Albert became very close to his younger sister Maria (he called her Maja) whose 1924 memoir remains our main source of information about his early life.

He apparently was slow to start speaking. Later on he would write that at the age of two or three he decided that he wanted to speak in complete sentences, which may explain the delay. (There is an old joke to the effect that his first words, at the age of three, were 'Father, there is something terribly wrong with the state of thermodynamics.')

Unfortunately, the feather-bed business did not prosper, and in 1880 the family moved to Munich where Hermann, in partnership with his younger brother, set up a business manufacturing electrical equipment. It was in Munich that, at the age of six, Albert started his formal schooling. Contrary to popular legend, he was a good student—there is a letter from his mother to his grandmother bragging that he was first in his class, for example. It was during this period that he began the study of the violin, a pastime that would play an important role in his public image later in life. In 1888 he moved on to a Gymnasium, where he would remain until he was 15. Again, contrary to the popular legend, he always received high marks in mathematics.

Although he was generally a good student, he was not particularly happy with the rigid, authoritarian teaching style that was the norm in Germany at the time. He also made few friends, showing an early inclination to become what his biographer Abraham Pais termed 'a man apart'. His most important educational experience, as he recounted later in life, was reading a book on Euclidean geometry and finding there an order and logical consistency that opened his mind. (I should point out that Euclid has played that same role in the lives of many boys who went on to become theoretical physicists, the author included.)

In 1894, the family business began to fail, and, leaving 16-year-old Albert behind to finish Gymnasium, the family moved to Italy, eventually settling in Pavia. Alone, depressed, and worried about compulsory military service, the young man left school and joined his family in Italy, planning to study on his own for the entrance exam to the *Eidgenössiche Technische Hochschule* (ETH) in Zurich, then as now one of the world's most prestigious technical universities. Although he did well in physics and math, he did not pass the exam, which included subjects like literary history and drawing. Consequently he took an alternate path to admission, enrolling at a school in Aarau to obtain a Matura (essentially a high school diploma). In 1896 he enrolled at the ETH and renounced his German citizenship (he became a Swiss citizen in 1901 and an American citizen in 1940).

At the ETH he made friends with fellow student Marcel Grossman, who would be important in his later life. Unfortunately, he apparently rubbed his professor, Heinrich Weber, the wrong way. Weber felt that Einstein, though bright, was too reluctant to take advice from others—not an uncommon failing in college students. In any case, when Einstein graduated in 1900 he was not offered a position as a teaching assistant at the ETH.

The next few years were difficult ones. Between periods of unemployment he had a couple of temporary teaching positions at what were essentially private high schools. This drought ended when Marcel Grossman's father brought him to the attention of the head of the Swiss patent office, with the result that in 1902 he was appointed as a patent examiner third class, his first permanent position and one that has lived on in the folklore of science. Shortly thereafter he married Mileva Marič, a woman who had been a fellow student in Zurich, and their first son was born in 1904.

Throughout this period Einstein found time to write a steady stream of physics papers, mostly about statistical mechanics. It was in 1905, however, a year often referred to as the *annus mirabilis* (year of wonders) in physics that he really came into his own. In that year he published four papers, any one of which could have earned him the Nobel Prize. Two of them, dealing with special relativity and mass–energy equivalence, will be discussed in later chapters. It is, I think, worthwhile to take a short detour to discuss the other two.

The photoelectric effect is a phenomenon that occurs when light (usually ultraviolet) is shone on a metal. As soon as the light is turned on, electrons start being ejected from the metal, and the energy of the electrons depends on the frequency (color) of the light—the higher the frequency the more energetic the electrons.

According to classical electrodynamics, there is no reason why electrons shouldn't be ejected because of the action of the light. Light, after all, consists partly of an electric field which can exert a force on electrons. The problem is that in the classical picture the effect should be analogous to surf washing a piece of driftwood ashore—it should happen slowly and should not depend on the frequency of the light.

Building on Max Planck's introduction of the idea of quantization, which will be discussed in the next chapter, Einstein suggested that light actually came in quanta as well—we now call these bundles of light 'photons'. (Planck had been unwilling to be so radical, and had only suggested that atoms absorbed and emitted light at specific frequencies while remaining agnostic as to the nature of light itself.) In this picture, the interaction between light and electrons is more like the collision between two billiard balls than surf washing driftwood ashore. In addition, the rules of quantization required that the higher the frequency of the light, the more energy the photon has and the more energy it can transmit to the electron. Thus, the introduction of the photon explained what is observed in the photoelectric effect.

This paper was one of the foundations of the developing field of quantum mechanics. In addition, it was the basis for the awarding of the Nobel Prize to Einstein in 1921—apparently relativity was still considered a bit too far out for the award at that time.

The other paper concerned a phenomenon known as Brownian motion. In 1827 the British botanist Robert Brown noticed that when a small particle like a pollen grain was suspended in a liquid and observed under a microscope, it jiggled around in an erratic kind of motion. Einstein realized that this obscure effect might be the solution to a long-standing debate about the nature of atoms. Throughout the nineteenth century, a debate had gone back and forth on the question of whether atoms were real, physical objects or whether matter just behaved as if it were made of atoms. In the latter case, of course, atoms would simply be mental constructs.

Einstein realized that if atoms were real, when one bounced off a pollen grain it would exert a tiny force—if the atom bounced to the right the grain would recoil to the left, for example. On average, as many atoms will hit on the left as on the right, so these forces would cancel out over time. Einstein noted, however, that at any given moment there could be more atoms hitting on one side of the grain than the other. Thus, the pollen grain would be subject to shifting forces, producing just the kind of erratic motion Brown had observed. Since mental constructs can't exert physical forces, this result was crucial in resolving the old debate.

In 1905, as well, Einstein completed his thesis (on molecular sizes) and was awarded a PhD at the University of Zurich. Not a bad output for a single year!

His reputation growing, Einstein started to move into academe. In 1908 he was appointed as a *privatdocent* at the University of Bern. This position allowed him to teach, but paid so little that he had to keep his day job at the patent office. It wasn't until 1909 that he obtained his first real faculty position—an associate professorship in theoretical physics at the University of Zurich. (We have records of faculty debates in which his future colleagues argue, in effect, that he was such a good scientist that the fact that he was Jewish should be ignored.) The position, of course, allowed him to resign from the patent office. Shortly thereafter, in 1910, his second son was born.

At Zurich, Einstein continued to publish papers in theoretical physics (11 papers in two years—an impressive output) and dabbled in experimental physics. Then, in a move that still puzzles his biographers, in 1911 he accepted a professorship at Karl Ferdinand University, a German language institution in Prague. He stayed there only a little over a year, and in 1912 he was back in Zurich, this time with a senior appointment at the ETH. It is clear that by this time Einstein had developed a growing reputation in the world of physics, and he received numerous inquiries from universities throughout Europe, garnering enthusiastic letters of support from luminaries like Max Planck and Marie Curie. Throughout this period, Einstein was also slowly working his way through the concepts that would result in the theory of general relativity, which we will discuss in Chapter 9.

This rapid hopping around between institutions was somewhat atypical of career paths in European universities at the time. It was much more common for people to enter a university as an undergraduate and remain at the same place, holding positions in graduate school, the junior faculty, and, eventually, the senior faculty. Today, however, Einstein's career track wouldn't look unusual at all. Physics students are routinely encouraged to apply for graduate training away from their undergraduate institutions and then, as often as not, will do post-doctoral fellowships at several other places before finally settling down. This kind of varied experience makes sense in a world in which all branches of science are becoming increasingly international.

In any case, after just three semesters in Zurich, Einstein left to take up a prestigious appointment in Berlin. The details of that appointment illustrate what a hot prospect the young theorist had become. His primary appointment was as a member of the Prussian Academy, but he was also made a professor at the University of Berlin, where he could teach if he wanted to, and promised the directorship of a new research lab. In fact, the promised new physics institute was created in the Kaiser Wilhelm Gessellschaft, a major research institute, in 1917. Even today, an appointment like this would be quite a plum. Einstein wrote to a friend 'I could not resist the temptation to accept a position which frees me of all obligations so that I can devote myself freely to thinking'.

Einstein would stay in Berlin until 1932. Unfortunately, soon after his arrival there he and Mileva separated, and she returned to Zurich with the boys. His professional life flourished, however. In 1915 he presented the field equations that make up the heart of general relativity to the Prussian Academy (the paper was published in 1916). Throughout the war years he continued to publish important papers. He also became involved with pacifist, and, to a lesser extent, Zionist organizations—political activities that would remain important throughout the rest of his life. Also, in 1919 he divorced Mileva (the divorce agreement stipulated that she would receive his Nobel Prize money, should it be awarded). He then married his distant cousin, Elsa Einstein Löwenthal, whom he had known since childhood.

During this period he also began what would be a lifelong project to present the results of his theories to the general public. In 1917, the publishers Vieweg in Braunschweig, Germany, published his popular book *On the Special and General Theories of Relativity*, a book that was to go through multiple expansions as time went on. The book was translated into English by Methuen publishers in London in 1920, and later brought out by Holt (now Holt, Rinehart, and Winston) in the United States. In 1993, Routledge brought the book out in its classic series, and this companion volume will be part of that long history.

The early Berlin years were full of what can only be described as professional administrative duties. In 1916 Einstein succeeded Max Planck as president of the German Physical Society (*Deutsche Physikalische Gessellschaft*), the society of professional physicists. He also served on boards of various scientific institutions in Germany and Holland. Then as now, these are the sorts of things you would expect for a man who was nearing the top of his profession. But as the war wound down, events were in motion that would change Einstein's life forever.

As we shall discuss in Chapter 13, general relativity makes predictions that can be verified experimentally. Einstein showed that the theory could explain a small but troubling anomaly in the orbit of Mercury, but, more importantly, he predicted that light passing near a massive body like the sun would be bent by a specified amount. The bending itself wasn't new—Newton had made a similar prediction—but the amount of predicted bending was (basically, relativity predicted twice as much deflection as did Newton). In those days, the only way this prediction could be verified was to observe stars near the sun during an eclipse. The war prevented several eclipse expeditions from being undertaken, but in 1919 the British astronomer (later Sir) Arthur Eddington was able to mount one. The details will be discussed in Chapter 13, but the result was stunning. Einstein's predictions were verified.

It's hard to overstate the effect this turn of events had on the life of someone the *New York Times* called 'the suddenly famous Dr Einstein'. Headlines blared 'Revolution in Science: Newton Overthrown', and Einstein became a household name all around the world. Historians have speculated about why this unusual 'canonization' occurred. Coming as it did at the end of World War I, the news broke on a populace that was weary, searching for a sign of hope. To people who had seen an entire generation of young men slaughtered senselessly in the trenches, the sudden appearance of a man who seemed to paint a new picture of the universe must have seemed little short of miraculous.

In addition, there seemed to be something almost magical about relativity—the legend that only a dozen men in the world understood it was born about this time. Given the outpouring of theoretical papers after 1919, that legend certainly wasn't true then, and it certainly isn't true today. Special relativity is routinely taught to tens of thousands of undergraduates every year, and the general theory to hundreds of graduate students. Human beings always need to sense a distance between themselves and their heroes, and the mathematical difficulty of general relativity seemed to provide just that sort of separation. Einstein's accomplishments seemed otherwordly, clouded in mystery. Popular descriptions of the man pictured him almost as a priest rather than a scientist. One biographer suggested that he was seen as a 'new Moses', bringing the word of God to humanity. In our modern world we can see a bit of this sort of attitude in the treatment of cosmologist Stephen Hawking.

Einstein was not only admired, but loved. A good illustration of this is an essay written by humorist Robert Benchley in 1936. Titled 'Taking up Cudgels', it can be found in his book *My Ten Years in a Quandary*. It is a hilarious 'defense' of general relativity against a competing theory, and concludes with these words addressed to the author of that theory:

> Who asked you to butt in on this? We were getting along very nicely with Prof. Einstein, who has proven himself to be an extremely pleasant gentleman... He also plays the violin. What do *you* play?

This veneration of Einstein culminated in 1999 when *Time Magazine* named him the 'person of the century', calling him 'the embodiment of pure intellect'.

In any case, Einstein enjoyed, but was not overwhelmed by, his newfound fame. Throughout the 1920s and early 1930s he traveled extensively, visiting the United States, South America, and Japan, among other places. As we shall see in Chapter 4, the visit to Japan has come to play a part in a minor scholarly debate about the genesis of special relativity. It was while he was en route to Japan, in fact, that he was notified that he would be awarded the Nobel Prize.

As we mentioned above, the Prize was not given for relativity, his most important contribution to science, but for his explanation of the photoelectric effect, one of the founding documents of the new field of quantum mechanics. This new science grew in stages. In 1913 the Danish physicist Niels Bohr (1885–1962) explained the behavior of the hydrogen atoms in quantum terms, and in the years that followed what is now known as the 'old' quantum theory was developed. We don't have the space to go into this in detail, but the central point was that it described the world inside the atom as a place where everything came in little bundles (quanta), but in which things like electrons could be thought of as something like miniature billiard balls in comforting analogy to the Newtonian world view. In 1925, however, the young German physicist Werner Heisenberg (1901–1976), joined later by the Austrian physicist Erwin Schrodinger (1887–1961), developed the modern version of quantum mechanics. The central differences between this new way of describing the world and the old, comfortable classical physics, were that (1) in the new quantum mechanics it is impossible to know two things about some pairs of quantities that describe a particle (its position and velocity, for example) with infinite precision, and (2) the properties of a particle (such as its position) can only be described in probabilistic terms. In other words, the old Newtonian idea that you can describe a billiard ball as being in a specific place and moving at a specific speed doesn't work in the quantum world. We have to say that the quantum billiard ball has a certain probability of being in various places and moving at various speeds. It was this proposition that caused Einstein to get off the quantum mechanics train.

It has always been something of a curiosity that a man who was one of the founders of quantum mechanics became one of its severest critics. These criticisms were played out dramatically in debates with Niels Bohr at what were called the Solvay conferences. (The conferences, held in Brussels starting in 1911, were sponsored by chemical manufacturer Ernest Solvay. They are still going on today.) It was at the 1927 Solvay Conference that Einstein delivered his famous 'God does not play dice' statement, a statement that expressed his dismay with the probabilistic interpretation of quantum mechanics described above. Less famous is Bohr's response—'Albert, stop telling God what to do.' This kind of playful badinage illustrates the fact that the two men were good friends and had a deep respect for each other.

The debate took on a stylized form. Einstein would propose a thought experiment that seemed to show that, for example, the position and velocity of a quantum particle could be determined simultaneously, despite the dictates of the new quantum mechanics. Bohr would go off and ponder the proposal and then come back to show why the experiment wouldn't work as Einstein predicted. In the end, Bohr usually prevailed and Einstein went back to the drawing board to try again.

In 1935, however, Einstein and his colleagues Boris Podolsky and Nathan Rosen published a paper that would have profound effects on the way people thought about quantum phenomena. The so-called EPR paper struck at one of the core principles of quantum mechanics—the idea that if a particle is not being measured it must be described as a probabilistic combination of all the states it could be in. For example, a quantum mechanical glove would have to be described as the sum of a certain probability of being right handed and another probability of being left handed.

The EPR argument was simple. Suppose (to use the above example) we knew that a particular system emitted two quantum mechanical gloves, and that there was some law that told us that if one glove was right handed the other had to be left handed. Suppose further that the system emitted two gloves, one going north and one going south, and we waited until the gloves were so far apart that light could not travel from one to the other in the time taken up by the experiment. Now suppose we measure the northward moving glove and find it is right handed. Then, EPR argued, we would know that the southward moving glove was left handed *even though we hadn't measured it.* EPR argued that this showed that there was a more complete description of the state than that given by quantum mechanics. This idea—that we could get back to a Newtonian picture if we could find the right description of the quantum state—came to be called the 'hidden variable' theory.

For a while EPR remained one of those unsolved puzzles that exist in every science. Then, in 1964, the Irish physicist John Bell (1928–1990) showed that there were experiments that would give different results if particles were described in terms of probabilities, as required by quantum mechanics, or described in terms of hidden variables (i.e. as having a definite state even though not being measured). In the 1970s several experimental groups actually carried out these experiments and the results were unequivocal; quantum mechanics was right and hidden variable theory was wrong.

The reason for this turn of affairs was that there is an unspoken assumption in the hidden variable argument presented above, and that is the assumption that the act of measurement is 'local'. In other words, we assume that making a measurement on the northward moving glove cannot affect the southward moving glove if they are separated as stated. It turns out that this assumption is wrong. When two particles (such as our gloves) are once described by a single probability distribution (as they are at the time of emission) they never stop being described that way. We say that they become 'entangled', so that measuring the northward moving glove does indeed affect the southward moving glove, even though no signal passes between them.

The concept of entanglement has generated what some authors call a 'second quantum mechanical revolution'. It is actually being developed to play a major role in cryptography and communication security. We can only wonder what Einstein would have made of this, but the concept of entanglement implicit in the EPR argument may have been his most important contribution to quantum mechanics.

Meanwhile, as all of this travel and work in physics went on, storm clouds were gathering in Germany. As early as 1920 ugly anti-Semitic incidents began to intrude on public and scientific discussions of relativity, to the point where some scientific meetings Einstein attended had to be guarded by the police. Nevertheless, during the 1920s Einstein enjoyed his life in Berlin, purchasing a summer cottage outside of the city and pursuing his hobby of sailing. In 1930 to 1932, he made two extended visits to the United States, spending his time at the California Institute of Technology in Pasadena. Because of his fame, he was frequently in the company of prominent scientists like Edwin Hubble as well as Hollywood personalities—he struck up a friendship with Charlie Chaplin, for example. There is a wonderful photograph of Einstein and his wife at the world premiere of *City Lights*, with Chaplin sitting between them.

The Nazis took over the Reichstag in July of 1932, and by this time Einstein had already realized that he would have to leave Germany. In December of that year the Einsteins left for their second trip to Cal. Tech. When they left their country home, Einstein is supposed to have stopped his wife and said 'Turn around. You will never see it again.' Indeed, he never again set foot in Germany.

The minute it became clear that Einstein was available, offers of professorships poured in from universities all over the world. There was a short period of travel, including stays in America, England, and Belgium (where the government had to supply him with a security detail because of the fear of Nazi assassins). While in the United State be began a series of conversations with Abraham Flexner, who was in the process of creating the Institute for Advanced Studies at Princeton, and eventually Einstein decided to make Princeton his home. When he started salary negotiations, he is supposed to have named a low salary, asking Flexner if he could live on less. Flexner is supposed to have replied 'Oh, I think we can do better than that.' Einstein's starting salary at the Institute was $15,000, which comes to about $2,500,000 in 2013 dollars, an amount matched in academe today only by university presidents and football coaches.

Before we go on to discuss Einstein's career at Princeton it is probably worthwhile to spend a few minutes contemplating the colossal stupidity of the Nazi regime in its treatment of science. Germany had spent several centuries creating the greatest university system the world had ever known. Anyone in the world who aspired to intellectual or scientific prominence had to spend time in Germany. The country's universities had much the same scientific status as American universities do today. And then, in a few years, the Nazis destroyed the entire system. When Max Planck, the senior scientific spokesman in the country, met with Hitler to warn him about the consequences of his policies, the reply he got was the quote at the beginning of this chapter.

One of the more bizarre manifestations of anti-Semitism in that country was the so-called *Deutsche Physik* movement. (Technically, this should be translated as 'German Physics', but is more often called 'Aryan Physics'.) The Aryan Physics movement wasn't some wacko fringe group. It was led by two Nobel Laureates, Philipp Lenard and Johannes Stark. Reading their manifestos is a strange experience—it's something like reading a physics textbook written by Richard Wagner. They really weren't for anything, as far as I can tell, but were clearly opposed to relativity, Einstein, and what they called 'Jewish physics'. I suppose it could be interpreted as a sort of left-handed compliment to Einstein that an entire movement was created to oppose his ideas.

At the scientific level, the movement was completely unsuccessful in its attempts to suppress relativity. Perhaps the best evocation of the men in this movement can be found in historian Russell McCormmach's novel *Night Thoughts of a Classical Physicist*. The novel explores the feelings of an older physicist in the early twentieth century, a man unable to understand the fundamental changes going on in his field or the younger men who were driving them. It's not hard to see that a physicist who had spent his career in the comfortable Newtonian world, surrounded by the luminiferous ether, would resent these newfangled ideas couched in complex mathematics coming from some punk kid at the patent office. I sometimes wonder whether some of my colleagues feel that way about string theory.

In any case, by 1933 Einstein was safely ensconced in Princeton, where he would spend the rest of his life. With the exception of the EPR paper discussed above, by this time his major contributions to physics were behind him. He played a small role in initiating the Manhattan Project during World War II, as we will discuss in Chapter 7, and was even offered the Presidency of the new state of Israel, which he wisely declined.

The physics problem that was at the center of his attention in those years is a deep one, and one that is still basically unsolved. I will state the problem here in its modern form and discuss it more fully in Chapter 14. It concerns the unification of forces, or what has come to be called unified field theory.

Today, physicists recognize four forces that are, singly or in concert, responsible for everything that happens in the universe. They are the familiar forces of electromagnetism and gravity—what I like to call the nineteenth-century forces—and the strong and weak forces, which operate only inside the nucleus—think of them as twentieth-century forces. The force you feel when you push on something, for example, is generated by the electrical forces between atoms in your hand and the thing you're pushing on. The strong force is what holds the nucleus together, while the weak force is responsible for some types of radioactive decay. The question is whether these forces are really distinct or whether they can be thought of as aspects of a single underlying unified force.

In the 1930s, the strong and weak forces were just starting to be understood (remember that the existence of the neutron wasn't proved until 1932), so Einstein concentrated his attention on gravity and electromagnetism. Despite repeated attempts to find a single theory that unified these two forces, he was ultimately unsuccessful. In Chapter 14 we will see that modern unified field theories do indeed unify three of the four forces—the electromagnetic, strong, and weak forces—in the so-called Standard Model. We shall see, however, that this formulation is entirely stated in quantum terms. Gravity, for which our best theory remains General Relativity, is essentially a force that depends on the geometry of space-time. As such, it has not yet been incorporated into a generally accepted theory with the other three forces. The split between quantum mechanics and relativity remains an important—some would say *the* important—unsolved problem in theoretical physics. As he did with the EPR paper, Einstein's work pointed the way toward the future of physics.

During the last years of his life, Einstein's health began to deteriorate due to the growth of an abdominal aneurism. He died on April 18, 1955. His statement to his doctors when he refused treatment near the end was simple: 'I have done my share; it is time to go. I will do it elegantly.'

2

THE STATE OF PHYSICS AT THE START OF THE TWENTIETH CENTURY

Nature and nature's laws lay hid in night;
God said 'Let Newton be' and all was light.

Alexander Pope

Before we can begin our exploration of Einstein's revolutionary theory of relativity, we should take some time to understand the way the world looked to physicists when he first came on the scene. The best way to picture the state of physics in 1900 is to imagine a three-legged stool. On the seat of the stool is one of the noblest products of the human mind, what we call the classical scientific world view. This view is supported by three sturdy pillars, three areas of science called mechanics (the science of motion), thermodynamics (the science of heat and energy) and the science of electricity and magnetism. We'll deal with each of these fields below, but here we simply make the point that they comprise a comprehensive picture of an orderly, predictable world. And, while the twentieth century was not particularly kind to this world view, as we shall see, it was the world from which Albert Einstein started.

In this chapter we shall examine the three pillars of classical physics separately, then turn to a strange narrative that has grown up about science at the start of the twentieth century. The narrative says, basically, that this was a time of complacency in science, when people believed that the basic laws that govern the universe were all known, and that all that was left was for scientists to determine the next decimal place. We will examine some contemporary documents to show that this narrative is not only wrong, but a complete misrepresentation of the world that Albert Einstein entered.

With these comments, let's turn to examining the three pillars of classical physics.

MECHANICS

Mechanics, as we said, is an old term for the study of motion. We can trace it far back in history, with Aristotle (384–322 BC) being one of the first thinkers to deal with it in a systematic way. Two central problems remained in this branch of science down through the millennia: the problem of acceleration and the problem of circular motion.

If you know that a car is traveling on a straight highway at 40 miles per hour, it doesn't take much insight to realize that thirty minutes from now it will be 20 miles away. This is a situation that will obtain whenever the speedometer needle on the car stays steady.

But what if the needle is moving? What if the car is accelerating or decelerating? Philosophers wrestled with this problem all through the middle ages, but it was Galileo Galilei (1564–1642) who finally worked out the answer. He didn't do it mathematically, but with an ingeniously designed experiment. He rolled brass balls down an inclined plane over which he had fastened something like guitar strings. As the ball passed each string it produced a 'ping', and Galileo adjusted the positions of the strings so that the time intervals between them were equal. (It turns out that the human ear is very good at distinguishing time intervals—Galileo, as a trained musician, could probably make his time intervals equal to an accuracy of 1/64th of a second.)

From his experiments, he was able to systematize the properties of accelerated motion. He found that the speed of an accelerated object increased linearly with time—the object was moving twice as fast after two seconds as it was after one second, for example. He also found that the distance traveled by an accelerating object increased as the square of the time—it had traveled four times as far after two seconds as it had after one, nine times as far after three seconds, and so on.

The problem of circular motion was harder, and Galileo never quite got it right. If you think of an object traveling in a circle—a ball being twirled around your head on a string, for example—it seems to be moving at the same speed all the time. Measure the distance the ball has traveled in any second and it will be the same as the distance it traveled in any other second. The point, though, is that the direction in which the ball is traveling changes at each point in its path. Physicists capture this difference by distinguishing between speed (distance traveled in a given time) and velocity (speed plus direction of travel). Thus, the ball is being accelerated (because its direction, and hence its velocity, changes) even though its speed is constant.

It was Isaac Newton (1642–1727) who finally put the science of mechanics on its modern footing. Born into a prosperous rural English family, he enrolled at Cambridge University just at the time the Black Plague was making one of its last visits to England. The university was closed for 18 months, and during this time the young Newton had nothing to do but think. He formulated the laws of motion and universal gravitation (described below), the theory of color, developed the differential and integral calculus, and proved a few random mathematical theorems. These were probably the most productive 18 months in the history of science. When I describe this period to my students, I always close by asking 'When I think about Newton at home all by himself, I have to ask myself what I accomplished last summer.'

Newton's Laws of Motion, in fact, can be thought of as the beginning of modern science. They are the laws that govern the motion of any object anywhere in the universe. They sound so simple that it's easy to miss their deep importance.

The First Law is:

> A particle will move in a straight line or remain at rest unless acted on by a force.

You can think of this law as telling us how to recognize when a force is acting. In the above example of a ball twirling on a string, it tells us that we have to apply a force to keep the ball moving in a circle. (You can convince yourself of this by thinking about what would happen if you let go of the string and stopped applying that force.)

The Second and Third Laws are:

The acceleration of a particle is directly proportional to the force and inversely proportional to the mass of the object.

and

For every action there is an equal and opposite reaction.

If the first law tells us when a force is acting, the second tells us what happens when a force acts, while the third tells us that forces always come in pairs.

As I said, these laws, as simple as they are, describe the motion of any object moving anywhere in the universe, from the rotation of a distant galaxy to the blood flowing in your veins. They do not, however, tell us anything about what forces exist. For this, we need extra information.

According to an account Newton gave later in his life, that information came about this way; he was walking in his parents' apple orchard one day and he saw an apple fall from a tree. At the same time, he saw the moon in the sky.

He knew that according to his laws, it was a force known as gravity that was acting on the apple, accelerating it downward. He also knew, from his First Law, that there had to be a force acting on the moon to keep it in orbit—otherwise it would just fly off in a straight line. He asked a question that seems simple and obvious to us now, but could only be asked for the first time by a genius. Could the force causing the apple to accelerate toward the ground be the same force that was holding the moon in orbit?

This inquiry eventually led to the final component of Newtonian mechanics, the Law of Universal Gravitation.

Between every two bodies in the universe there is an attractive force proportional to their masses and inversely proportional to the square of the distance between them.

Double the mass of an object, in other words, and you double the force of gravity it exerts. Move it twice as far away and the force drops to a quarter of its value. (I should add that there is a mild disagreement among scholars over the question of whether Newton actually worked these things out in the orchard, when he said he did, or whether he told this story later to establish intellectual priority.)

Applying Newton's Laws of Motion to a system in which gravity operates should explain things like the orbits of the planets in the solar system, and indeed, scientists spent centuries after Newton carrying out these sorts of calculations in ever greater detail. More importantly, though, the picture of the universe implicit in Newton's thought had impacts in all areas of science—it essentially produced a template that told people how to go about answering scientific questions. It established the procedure that has been in use since then, the procedure that requires that every theory be verified by observation or experiment before it is accepted.

The point is that Newton gave us a picture of an orderly, predictable universe. The phenomena we see can be thought of as being analogous to the hands of a clock. What Newton demonstrated was that human beings, using their minds, can penetrate to the clockwork underneath the observed phenomena, and, as he saw it, discover what was in the mind of God when he set the entire universe in motion. I call the working out of this vision the 'Newtonian Project'.

This orderly mechanical picture of the universe had profound effects in many areas outside of science as well. Its influence can be seen in music and literature, for example, and there are even scholars who argue that the men who created the constitution of the United States were deeply influenced by Newtonian ideas. In Chapter 6 we will also see that some aspects of the Newtonian world view were crucial in the development of Einstein's theory of relativity.

THERMODYNAMICS

Aside from constituting an important background for Einstein's famous equation $E = mc^2$, which we will discuss in Chapter 7, the science of thermodynamics had little direct bearing on the development of the theory of relativity. Nevertheless, it played an important role in creating the Newtonian world view.

Think about what happened when you lifted this book. You exerted a force equal to the weight of the book over a distance of a foot or so. In the jargon of physics, you did work—an amount of work equal to the force you exerted multiplied by the distance over which that force was applied. Energy is defined as the ability to do work (i.e. to exert a force over a distance). We shall see in Chapter 7 that there are three important statements that can be made about energy:

- Energy comes in many forms.
- Energy can be shifted from one form to another.
- The total energy of a closed system cannot change over time.

The third statement is called the First Law of Thermodynamics, and is often stated in the form:

- The total energy of a closed system is conserved.

The discovery of the laws governing energy in the mid-nineteenth century had a profound effect on many areas of science. For example, the sun is pouring out energy continuously (you can feel it on your face on a warm day). The law tells us that this energy has to come from somewhere. This meant that for the first time astronomers had to confront the question of where a star's energy came from—a question that wasn't answered until the 1930s. At a deeper level, they had to confront the fact that whatever the energy source of the sun and other stars was, it would someday be exhausted. Stars, like everything else in the universe, are born and die.

The other side of the thermodynamic coin is called the Second Law. It deals with another aspect of the universe—its temporal directionality. In principle, it should take as much energy to unscramble an omelet as to scramble it, but we know that the latter process is easy while the former is not. The Second Law deals with the amount of order in a system (physicists refer to this as 'entropy'). The Law basically says that closed systems cannot become more ordered spontaneously.

Because this law is so frequently misunderstood, I would like to point out that the law does *not* say that systems cannot become more ordered over time. It just says that they can do so only if energy is supplied from the outside. For example, your refrigerator routinely converts liquid water (a disordered system) into ice cubes (which are highly ordered). It can do so because energy is being supplied by a power plant somewhere. In fact, my personal favorite way of stating the Second Law is 'A refrigerator won't work unless it's plugged in.' The disorder at the power plant, balanced against the order in the ice cube, guarantees that the entire system (ice cube plus power plant) becomes more disordered, as required by the Second Law. I bring this up because Creationists frequently argue that highly ordered living systems could not have arisen spontaneously without violating the Second Law—a totally fallacious argument.

ELECTRICITY AND MAGNETISM

As we shall see in Chapter 6, it was the formulation of the laws of electricity and magnetism by Scottish physicist James Clerk Maxwell (1831–1879) in 1861 that played a crucial role in the development of relativity. The phenomena of electricity and magnetism were both known to philosophers in the ancient world. The Greeks, for example, knew that if you rubbed a piece of amber with cat's fur and then touched the amber to small bits of material like cork, those bits would repel each other. Today we call this phenomenon static electricity. (As an aside, we should note that the word 'electricity' is derived from 'elektros', the Greek word for amber.) They also knew that if you rubbed a piece of glass with silk and touched those bits of cork, they would repel each other as well. Bring a bit of cork touched by amber near a bit of cork touched by glass, however, and the bits are attracted.

In modern language, we say that there are two kinds of electrical charge, which were given the names 'positive' and 'negative' by the American statesman and scientist Benjamin Franklin (1706–1790). (Incidentally, had Nobel Prizes been in existence in the eighteenth century, Franklin would certainly have gotten one for his pioneering work in electricity.) The actual law that describes the electrical force was worked out in a series of experiments by the French scientist Charles-Augustin de Coulomb (1736–1806). The law says that like charges repel each other, while unlike charges attract. The magnitude of the force obeys an equation that bears an uncanny resemblance to the Law of Universal Gravitation, a point to which we will return in Chapter 14. The force between two charged objects is proportional to the product of the charges and inversely proportional to the distance between those charges. The important quantity for us is the number that relates the size of those two charges and the distance between them to the size of the resulting force, a quantity called the 'proportionality constant'. Tell me the size of the charges and the distance between them, in other words, and the proportionality constant will allow me to calculate the force. As a result of his experiments, Coulomb was able to assign a number to the proportionality constant in his law, a fact that would play a crucial role in the development of relativity.

Like electricity, the phenomenon of magnetism was known to the ancients, mainly because there are naturally occurring minerals, such as lodestones, that act as magnets and can be used as compasses to aid navigation. The English physician William Gilbert (1544–1603) conducted a series of experiments that established the facts that (1) the Earth acts as a giant magnet, and (2) magnets have two poles (labeled north and south), and (3) like poles repel while unlike poles attract. From our point of view, the most important result of Gilbert's work is the finding that there are no isolated magnetic poles in nature—whenever you find a north pole you find a south pole associated with it and vice versa.

So by the beginning of the nineteenth century, these two phenomena were well understood. There seemed to be, however, no connection between them. In modern terms, why should a sock sticking to a towel when you take it out of the dryer (a result of static electricity) have anything to do with notes stuck onto your refrigerator with a magnet? This state of affairs, however, was about to change.

It began in a lecture hall at the University of Copenhagen, where physicist Hans Christian Oersted (1777–1851) was demonstrating a new device. He would have called it an 'electric pile', but we would call it a battery. It was a device that could produce a flow of electrical charge, rather than just a static accumulation of charge. Oersted noticed that whenever current was flowing in his apparatus, a nearby magnet changed direction. He found, in other words, that moving electrical charges can exert magnetic forces. In the jargon of physics, he found that electrical currents produce magnetic fields. Thus, the two seemingly disparate phenomena of electricity and magnetism were actually found to be connected.

The second piece of the puzzle was supplied by the English physicist Michael Faraday (1791–1867). The simplest way to picture Faraday's discovery is to imagine a loop of wire on a table, with no battery or other power source connected. If a magnet is moved around near that loop, Faraday found that as long as the magnet is moving, a current will flow in the wire. A changing magnetic field, in other words, will produce an electric current. He also found that changing the area or orientation of the loop while holding the magnet fixed had the same effect. This result is the basic working principle of the electrical generator, the device that produces virtually all of the electricity used by modern societies.

By the middle of the nineteenth century, then, we had found that electricity and magnetism are intimately related to each other—two sides of the same coin. This connection is reflected in the term 'electromagnetism' that we will use throughout the rest of this book.

It was at this point that James Clerk Maxwell came on the scene. He added a small term to Oersted's results, but, more importantly, he realized that the above results form a coherent mathematical whole. These laws are known today as Maxwell's Equations, and they play the same role in electromagnetism that Newton's Laws do in mechanics and the Laws of Thermodynamics do in the science of energy and entropy. To summarize, Maxwell's Equations are:

- Like charges repel, unlike charges attract, according to Coulomb's law.
- There are no isolated magnetic poles.
- Electrical currents produce magnetic fields.
- Changing magnetic fields produce electrical currents.

ELECTROMAGNETIC RADIATION

From the point of view of the development of relativity, the most important result of Maxwell's Equations is that they predict the existence of waves that are composed of oscillating electric and magnetic fields. Scientists had known about waves for centuries—think of ripples on a pond as an example. Maxwell showed that the above equations predicted a similar phenomenon, except that instead of water moving up and down as in a ripple, it was electric and magnetic fields that were growing and diminishing. Much more importantly, though, he showed that the speed of these new waves was related to the experimentally determined strength of the forces between electrical charges and between magnets—what we called the 'proportionality constant' above. When Maxwell plugged in the numbers, he found that the speed of his new electromagnetic waves was 186,000 miles per second. This was known to be the speed of light, of course, and this was Maxwell's great surprise—light itself is an electromagnetic wave. Today we know that everything from radio waves (with wavelengths many miles long) to gamma rays (with wavelengths smaller than the nucleus of an atom) are electromagnetic waves. They all travel at the same speed and differ from each other only in the magnitude of their wavelengths. The speed of these waves is so important that it is given a special designation—'c'. The most important thing about c is that it is built into Maxwell's Equations, and hence into the laws of nature themselves. We shall return to this point repeatedly.

All the waves that physicists had encountered up to this time required a medium to travel in. Ripples move on water, seismic waves in rock, sound waves in the air. And this naturally leads to a question: What was the medium on which these newly discovered waves moved?

To answer this question, scientists turned to an old idea—the ether—that goes back at least as far as Aristotle. This was supposed to be a thin substance that permeated the universe, and it was natural to say that electromagnetic waves were perturbations in the ether in much the same sense that sound waves are perturbations in the air.

Fair enough, but in 1887 two scientists at what is now Case-Western Reserve University in Cleveland conducted an experiment that called the whole idea of the ether into question. Albert Michelson (1852–1931) and Edward Morley (1838–1923) realized that there was a simple way to monitor the motion of the Earth through the ether. The key point is that if the ether is stationary, then the motion of the Earth in its orbit would create an 'ether wind' in much the same way as the motion of a car creates a wind on a still day. Furthermore, that wind should be different at different times of year—different in June and January, for example, because the Earth is moving in different directions—so that there should be an annual modulation which would affect the speed of light at the Earth's surface. Michelson and Morley used a sensitive optical system to search for this change in speed, but found nothing. Today, of course, we realize that the null result was only to be expected, since there is no such thing as the ether. At the time, however, this experiment was seen as a major and unexplained discrepancy in the classical world picture.

THE COMPLACENCY NARRATIVE

As we mentioned above, there is a common narrative about the state of science at the beginning of the twentieth century, a narrative that seriously distorts the context of Einstein's development of the theory of relativity. The narrative goes something like this: during the nineteenth century, scientists completed work on the three great pillars of classical physics—mechanics, electricity and magnetism, and thermodynamics. Because of this, the narrative continues, by the start of the twentieth century, a sense of smug complacency had settled over the scientific world, and the general feeling was that all that was left was for scientists to work out the details, determine the next decimal place.

I have to admit that I have always been skeptical about this narrative. For one thing, there were tremendously exciting things going on in physics at the time. J.J. Thomson (1856–1940) discovered the electron in 1897, at the same time that Marie Sklodowska Curie (1867–1934) was opening up the study of radioactivity which would eventually develop into the field of nuclear physics—work that would make her the first person to be awarded two Nobel Prizes in science. The new science of quantum mechanics was inaugurated in 1900, when Max Planck (1858–1947) introduced the notion of quantum behavior at the atomic level. With all of this going on, it's hard to see how anyone could be complacent.

Furthermore, there is a kind of natural cantankerousness in the scientific character. Scientists are taught to question everything, to probe accepted ideas until they break down. It's just hard for me to imagine a scientist settling back into an easy chair and deciding that the game was over.

Nevertheless, those who buy into the complacency narrative usually cite a statement supposed to have been made by Lord Kelvin, arguably the greatest scientist of his time, at a meeting of the British Association for the Advancement of Science in 1900:

> There is nothing new to be discovered in physics now. All that remains is more and more precise measurement.

Unfortunately, this seems to be a situation in which a statement has slipped into common acceptance without anyone checking to see if the quotation is accurate. A number of scholars have tried (and failed) to find contemporary references to it, which makes its attribution to Kelvin questionable at best.

In fact, we do have an extensive discussion of Kelvin's views on the state of physics in 1900. In the *Proceedings of the Meetings of the Members of the Royal Institution of Great Britain* (Vol XVI, 1899–1901, p. 363) we find an address given by Kelvin at a weekly evening meeting held on Friday, April 27, 1900, summarizing and extending a lecture he had given earlier. Titled *19th Century Clouds on the Dynamical Theory of Heat and Light*, it states

> The beauty and clearness of the dynamical theory, which asserts heat and light to be modes of motion, is at present obscured by two clouds.

The 'dynamical theory' was what we call classical physics, and the 'two clouds' were (1) the problem of the ether, and (2) the problem of something called the equipartition of energy, which led to a result that physicists labeled the 'ultraviolet catastrophe'. Let's look at these one at a time.

As we have said, in order to make sense of electromagnetic phenomena like light and radio waves, physicists at the end of the nineteenth century imagined that space was filled with a tenuous material they called ether, with electromagnetic waves moving through the ether more or less like sound waves moving through the air. Kelvin spends a lot of time worrying about how objects can actually move through the ether, but then gets to the real heart of the problem. In that famous experiment discussed above, Albert Michelson and Edward Morley had showed that there was no evidence that the Earth was actually moving through something like the ether. Kelvin commented that he could 'find no fault' with either the conceptualization or the execution of the experiment, but was clearly puzzled by the result. One conclusion we can draw from the experiment, of course, is that there is no ether. Kelvin didn't go that far, but concludes with the following statement:

I'm afraid cloud #1 is very dense.

The discussion of the second 'cloud' centers around the statement that for a system in thermal equilibrium, energy will be shared among the different forms of energy (e.g. kinetic and rotational) available to the system. Kelvin concentrates primarily on problems in what we would today call kinetic theory, but the main historical importance of this theorem come from the fact that when it is applied to radiation trapped in a container, it leads to an impossible result. Essentially, because there are an infinite number of vibrational modes available to the radiation, the total energy of the system would have to be infinite. This was called the 'ultraviolet catastrophe' at the time, because the infinite number of wavelengths that can fit into the box (think harmonics) build up in the high frequency (ultraviolet) part of the spectrum. Again, Kelvin had no suggestions about how to resolve this problem.

What was amazing to me as I read through Kelvin's talk was that he had put his finger precisely on the points that would lead to the two major revolutions in twentieth-century physics. The absence of the ether meant, in essence, that there was no privileged, 'God's eye' frame of reference from which to view physical phenomena. This, of course, was the starting point of Einstein's development of the theory of relativity. Ironically, in 1900, the same year as Kelvin's lecture, the German physicist Max Planck showed that the ultraviolet catastrophe could be resolved if we assume that atoms can emit radiation only in discrete bundles he called 'quanta'. This was the beginning of the development of quantum mechanics, the second great revolution of the twentieth century.

Some authors have suggested that Kelvin regarded his 'clouds' as minor details to be cleaned up before everything would be known. I have to say that I don't get that impression from the talk. Although I'm certain that Kelvin thought his problems would be solved in the framework of classical physics, his comment about the 'dense cloud' shows he found these issues truly puzzling. Besides, you don't write a 40-page lecture about trivial details!

3

COORDINATE SYSTEMS
EINSTEIN'S *RELATIVITY* CHAPTERS 1–4

Things equal to the same thing are equal to each other.

Euclid

In these chapters, Einstein introduces the notion of coordinate systems, paying special attention to coordinate systems defined in terms of rigid bodies. He also discusses the nature of mathematical truths and introduces what he calls the 'Galilean' coordinate system, in which an object not being acted on by a force moves in a straight line.

Where are you right now?

This seems to be an easy enough question to answer—'I'm at home', or 'I'm at the library' or whatever. But of course that answer leads immediately to another, deeper question: where, exactly, is 'home' or 'the library' or wherever else you are? Let's pose this question in a somewhat unorthodox way—how would you communicate your position right now to an extraterrestrial alien approaching Earth in a spaceship?

You could start by looking at your GPS system, which would give you two numbers—latitude and longitude. These will start to pinpoint your location, but they would leave something out. With only these two numbers, the alien wouldn't know of you were in an airplane flying over your house at 30,000 feet, on the ground, or in a deep tunnel under your house. To remove this ambiguity, you'd have to supply a third number, such as altitude (your height above sea level). These three numbers would locate your house precisely, but they still wouldn't answer the question completely, because it wouldn't say when 'right now' is. To complete the job, you would have to supply a fourth number, the time. If you told the alien 'I am at this latitude, this longitude, and this elevation at 10 a.m. on Tuesday morning', he, she, or it would know precisely where you are and when you are there. (To be precise, we would have to complete this description by defining the unit of measurement we're using—it makes a difference whether you're one foot or one mile above sea level.)

This is a simple exercise in dealing with what are called coordinate frames. In this case three numbers—latitude, longitude, and altitude— define a location. We generally refer to each of these as a 'dimension'. If we add the time, we have defined an 'event'—something that occurred at a given place at a given time. (Incidentally, this is all that is involved in the standard science fiction ploy of referring to time as the 'fourth dimension'.)

As we shall see in the next chapter, the specification of a coordinate system is the first step in defining a frame of reference, a description of the place from which someone observes the world. Frames of reference are a central concept in developing the theory of relativity.

It is a characteristic of coordinate systems that locations are defined in terms of numbers—one number for each dimension. For example, I am writing this in my favorite coffee shop in the suburbs of Washington DC. I would define my location by saying that I am at (approximately) 38 degrees north latitude, 77 degrees west longitude, and 410 feet above sea level—latitude, longitude, and altitude. Add the time and I would have defined the event of writing these words.

We can learn some general features of coordinate systems by thinking a bit more about this example. Longitude is the angle between two planes—a plane passing through the Earth's center, the North Pole, and Washington DC and a plane passing through the Earth's center, the North Pole, and the Royal Observatory at Greenwich, outside of London.

Why Greenwich?

Why not? You have to start counting somewhere, and for various historical reasons the Observatory at Greenwich was chosen for what is called the 'Prime Meridian'. This illustrates an important point about coordinate systems—the place where you start counting, the 'zero', is arbitrary. Once the zero has been chosen, however, the number assigned to each location is fixed.

Similarly, latitude is defined to be the angle up from the equator to the pole in each hemisphere and altitude is defined as the distance above sea level. The arbitrariness of these choices is particularly evident in the case of altitude, since the Earth's sea level changes constantly. It was significantly lower, for example, during the last Ice Age, when a large fraction of the planet's water was taken into glaciers, and has been rising at a rate of about 18 cm (about seven inches) per century ever since.

Having said this, however, we have to note that some things about coordinate systems do not depend on arbitrary choices. The numbers you assign to the coordinates giving the location of two places (London and Washington DC, for example) may depend on your choice of the zero of longitude, but the distance between the two locations will not. Set the Prime Meridian in Moscow, Beijing, or Kansas City and the distance between London and Washington DC will be the same.

Here's a simple example to illustrate this point. The longitude of Greenwich is 0 (by convention), and the longitude of Washington DC is about 77 degrees west. This means that the angular difference between the two is 77 − 0 = 77 degrees. (From this fact and the known radius of the Earth we could work out the distance between the two places if we wanted to.)

Now suppose that the Prime Meridian were set in Paris, as some wanted it to be in the past. Paris is now about 2 degrees east longitude, so if we shifted the Prime Meridian, the longitude of Greenwich would be 2 degrees west and the longitude of Washington DC would be 79 degrees west. The angular separation between London and Washington would then be 79 − 2 = 77 degrees—exactly the same as what it is when the Prime Meridian is in Greenwich.

As a historical aside, we should note that there have been many different choices made for the Prime Meridian over time. The Alexandrian scientist Eratosthenes (~276–195 BC) is generally credited with putting forward the idea of longitude, but it was his successor Claudius Ptolemy (~90–168 AD) who produced the first world map that contained a Prime Meridian. It was located out in the Atlantic, in something called the 'Fortunate Isles' (probably the Canaries). Apparently he wanted the Meridian far out to sea, away from all land. Christopher Columbus noted that there was a point in the Atlantic where compass needles pointed due north and suggested that for the Prime Meridian. (Today we would say that this was a line drawn between the geographic North Pole and the magnetic North Pole.) In 1634, Cardinal Richelieu in France introduced a system in which Paris was the *de facto* Prime Meridian, but between 1765 and 1811 the English astronomer Nevil Maskelayne produced a series of handbooks for navigators in which the Meridian was at his home base at the Royal Observatory in Greenwich. These handbooks became so popular that by 1884, when an international conference was held in Washington DC to deal with the question of specifying the Prime Meridian, Greenwich was the hands down choice. (We should note that the only holdouts at the conference were the French, who first proposed a neutral line drawn through the Bering Straits and then kept using their old Paris-based system until 1911.)

Although you might think that Columbus' suggestion for the Prime Meridian has some physical basis, it would have been a poor choice. The North Magnetic Pole actually wanders around on a timescale of years, so this choice would have led to a wandering Meridian. At least Greenwich pretty much stays in one place.

The familiar system of latitude, longitude, and altitude is actually an example of what mathematicians call 'polar' coordinates. It is a very convenient way of dealing with points on the surface of a sphere like the Earth. From the point of view of geometry, however, it is something of a late-comer on the scene. Nevertheless, it is a system in which we can assign numbers to points (such as Washington DC and Greenwich) on the surface of a rigid body such as the Earth. This, in fact, is where Einstein starts his discussion of coordinate systems.

The most familiar kind of geometry—the kind of stuff we all learned in school—deals with points on a flat plane, which are much easier for us to visualize and with which humans have had a great deal of experience. Before going into the history of plane geometry, however, we should take a moment to discuss a point that Einstein brings up tangentially, and that is the question of what it means for a mathematical statement to be 'true'.

As we shall see when we examine the work of Euclid below, mathematical systems are laid out in a special way. There are a series of axioms or postulates and then a series of propositions that can be proved from those postulates. In such a system, a proposition is 'true' if it follows in a logical way from the axioms. For example, we will see below that the statement 'the angles in a triangle add up to 180 degrees' is 'true' in the sense that it follows from Euclid's axioms.

This sense of 'true' has to be very carefully separated from the question of whether or not the description in a particular geometrical system corresponds to anything in the real world. That is not a question that can be answered in the mathematical system itself, for the simple reason that it involves observations. For example, the latitude-longitude-altitude coordinate system is a simple way of describing locations on the surface of a perfect sphere. Calculations such as determining the distance between two points mentioned above are easy in this idealized situation. Similarly, many mathematical theorems can be proved for the surface of an ideal sphere.

In point of fact, however, the Earth is not a perfect sphere—it bulges at the equator because of its spin. This fact has nothing to do with the mathematical properties of a perfect sphere—it just means that those properties don't apply on the Earth.

This is, in fact, a good example of the difference between mathematics and a science like physics. To prove a statement in a mathematical system, you have to demonstrate that it follows from the system's axioms. To prove a statement in physics, you have to show that it is consistent with observations of the real world. We can capture this difference by saying that mathematics deals with logical systems, while sciences like physics deal with empirical ones.

With this understood, we can turn to investigating the development of our understanding of geometry and mathematics over time.

Today the field of forefront mathematics is an abstract affair, pursued primarily by reclusive professors in university departments. It wasn't always this way, though. In its origins, mathematics was an intensely practical business, developed because of its usefulness. The first step was certainly the development of a number system.

The acquisition of counting by humans is lost in the mists of antiquity, but we know that all of the ancient civilizations had number systems. Roman numerals are most familiar to western readers, but they are a comparatively late development. The earliest number system we know about appeared in Egypt over 5000 years ago. It was a simple system, similar to Roman numerals. A line stood for 'one', an inverted U for 'ten', a coil something like a backward '9' for 'one hundred', a lotus for a 'thousand' and so on. They also developed a rough version of geometry, as we shall see below. We actually know a lot about Egyptian mathematics because several papyrus manuscripts of mathematical textbooks have survived to the present.

Actually, it's not surprising that the Egyptians had a mathematical system. How could you even think about building something like the pyramids if you couldn't count? Or re-survey your fields after the annual flood if you knew nothing of geometry? Besides, numbers mattered to the Egyptians, who were what one author called a 'nation of accountants'. There is a story (which I hope is apocryphal) that they counted their dead enemies after a battle by creating a pile of severed penises.

The Sumerians and Babylonians also developed a complex mathematical system. It was interesting because it was a based on the number 60, rather than the number 10 as our system is. In other words, while we count to 9 before moving over a place and writing a one and a zero (a 10), a Babylonian would count to 59 before writing the equivalent to 10 in their system. No one knows why they used base 60, but vestiges of that system survive today. Have you ever wondered why there are 360 degrees in a circle or 60 minutes in a hour? Blame it on the Babylonians.

The development of coordinate systems depends on having a number system, of course, but it also depends on a knowledge of geometry. As was mentioned above, this was a field of mathematics that the Egyptians had to develop early on because of the nature of their relationship with the Nile. Until the recent construction of the high dam at Aswan, the Nile would flood every year, overlaying fields with fresh, fertile soil. This made Egypt the breadbasket of the Mediterranean world, a fact reflected in the remark of the historian Herodotus that Egypt was the 'gift of the Nile'. The annual need to re-survey their fields, along with the basic engineering knowledge needed to construct monuments like their temples and pyramids, drove the Egyptians to develop a kind of rough and ready geometry.

The Rhind Papyrus is named for the Scottish antiquarian A. Henry Rhind, who purchased the papyrus in Luxor in 1858 and left it to the British Museum. It is a mathematics textbook written in about 1650 BC. We can get a good sense of the way the Egyptians approached geometry by looking at one of the problems in the text.

A field round of khet (diameter) nine. What is the amount (area) thereof?

Here is how the student is told to solve the problem:

> Take thou away 1/9 of it, namely 1. Remainder is 8. Make thou the multiplication 8×8. Becomes it 64. The amount of it, this is the area.

In modern language, this means that the Egyptian formula for the area of a circle is

$$A = (8/9\ d)^2 = (16/9\ r)^2 = 3.160 r^2$$

where r is the radius of the circle. But we all learned in grade school that the correct formula for the area of a circle is

$$A = \pi r^2 = 3.14159\ldots r^2$$

The Egyptians, in other words, developed a way of calculating the area of a circle that was accurate to 1 percent and for them *that was good enough*. They really weren't interested in understanding any deep truths about mathematical systems—they just wanted to get their fields re-surveyed and planted. It would never occur to them to calculate π to millions of decimal places, as has been done today. The Egyptian preoccupation with practical outcomes is reflected in everything we know about their mathematics. They had all sorts of 'good enough' ways of calculating things like the areas of odd-shaped fields, the capacity of silos, and the slopes of pyramids.

This kind of mathematics is very different from that developed by the Greeks and used by scientists like Isaac Newton and Albert Einstein. Our modern style of mathematics can be traced back to the Alexandrian scholar Euclid (~300 BC) who is generally credited with compiling the most influential mathematics text ever written, the *Elements*.

Some background: Alexandria was (and is) a port city located where a branch of the Nile delta empties into the Mediterranean. It was one of a couple of dozen cities called 'Alexandria' that were founded in territories conquered by Alexander the Great (356–323 BC). It served as the governmental center of Egypt until 30 BC, after which it became a major Roman provincial capital. Although it was located in Egypt, it was in fact a Greek city, a center of Hellenistic culture. One author called it a 'gated community', which pretty well summarizes what it was. For example, the last Greek ruler of the city, Cleopatra (69–30 BC) (yes, *that* Cleopatra) was the first of her line to bother to learn the Egyptian language.

Oddly enough, given his importance, we actually know very little about Euclid's life. We don't know when or where he was born or when he died. There is even a mild debate among scholars about whether he actually wrote the *Elements*, since that attribution was made by scholars hundreds of years after his death. According to legend, when one of the Alexandrian rulers asked him if there was an easy way to learn mathematics, Euclid is supposed to have replied 'There is no royal road to geometry'. And that's pretty much it—all we know about the man who (probably) wrote one of the most important books in history.

What made *Elements* so important was not that it contained new results—most of what Euclid included had been discovered by other scholars. He includes, for example, a proof of the Pythagorean theorem, a result that had been known for hundreds of years by the time of his writing.

Euclid begins by setting down a set of what he called 'common notions' and 'postulates'. Today we would call these 'definitions' and 'axioms'. For example, under common notions he defines things like points and lines— simple constructs that will be needed in any discussion of geometry. The postulates include statements like the quote at the opening of this chapter, but the most important postulate from our point of view—postulate 5— requires a little thought. What it says, basically, is that if you have a line and a point outside of the line, then it is possible to draw one and only one line through that point that will be parallel to the original line.

Sounds reasonable, doesn't it? Intuitively, you can see that if you tip that parallel line by the tiniest amount and extend it far enough, it will eventually intersect the original line. The only line that won't do this is the one that is parallel. For our purposes, this postulate is the defining feature of what has come to be called Euclidean geometry. It is a postulate that will be true on a plane surface.

Once the postulates are in place, we can begin proving theorems. Just to give a sense of what this process is like, let me take a moment to prove that the sum of the angles in a triangle add up to 180 degrees in the Euclidean style.

Consider Figure 3.1. From postulate 5, we know that we can draw a line through the apex of the triangle which is parallel to the base, as shown. From previous theorems we also know that opposite angles like the two

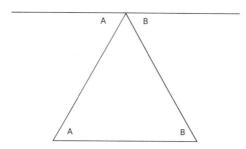

Figure 3.1 Diagram used in proving that the sum of the angles of a triangle add up to 180 degrees

labeled 'A' and the two labeled 'B' are equal to each other, although A and B are not, in general, equal to each other. Thus the three angles at the apex—the ones labeled 'A', 'B', and the apex angle itself—represent the sum of the angles in the triangle. But since (by construction) the line through the apex is straight, the angles have to add up to 180 degrees. At this point we write QED (it stands for *Quod Erat Demonstrandum*, or 'as was to be demonstrated').

Other proofs may be more complex, but they all follow this basic pattern. We start with the basic postulates (postulate 5 in the above example) and work our way through a series of logical steps to an inescapable conclusion. It is the crystalline clarity of this method that so impressed the young Albert Einstein, as discussed in a previous chapter. It also set a standard for the presentation of mathematical and scientific results that we still honor today. If you read Isaac Newton's *Principia*, for example, you can see that it is clearly modeled on Euclid.

The Euclidean system forms a complete logical whole. Once the axioms are given, all of the theorems follow. It describes, as we said, the geometry of a flat plane, and for most of mathematical history since Euclid, it was assumed that it was the only possible geometry that there could be. Before we go on to examine this point, however, let's explore the Euclidean world a little more.

In the seventeenth century the world of geometry was enriched by the French philosopher and mathematician René Descartes (1596–1650). Descartes is best known for his famous philosophical dictum *Cogito ergo sum* (I think, therefore I am), but in fact he was a major figure in the development of modern mathematics as well.

For starters, he introduced what is called the Cartesian coordinate system. You can picture it this way: imagine a line running from left to right in the plane of this book (this is usually called the 'x axis'). Imagine another line (the 'y axis') running up and down in the plane of the book, making a right angle with the x axis. Finally, imagine a third line (the 'z axis') coming up out of the page at right angles from the point at which the x and y axes intersect. These three lines can then be used to define the position of any point in space. For example, you could define a point by saying 'Go three units to the right on the x axis, two units up on the y axis, and five units up on the z axis'. We would write the location of this point as (3, 2, 5). In this way, every point in space corresponds to a triplet of numbers.

Cartesian coordinates seem to be a very natural way of representing points on a plane (i.e. points for which $z = 0$). An amusing application of this naturalness can be seen by looking at the street grids of European and American cities. The older sections of European cities grew organically, and tend to have winding streets and picturesque intersections. In the nineteenth century, however, when many American cities were being built, it was felt that the Cartesian system was the only rational way for a city to be organized. Consequently, cities were laid out in a Cartesian grid. In my home town of Chicago, for example, the grid is oriented so that one set of streets runs north and south while another set runs east and west. The point we could designate as (0, 0) is an arbitrarily chosen corner in the business district (State and Randolph, if you must know) and every other location is defined by a number designating the distance north or south you would have to go from that corner to get to the location you want, and another number designating how far east or west. For example, Wrigley Field, the home of the Chicago Cubs baseball team, is located 36 blocks north and 10 blocks west of that central intersection. Next time you fly into an American city, see if you can discern the influence of that seventeenth-century French philosopher.

As an aside, we should note that the choice of the point designated (0, 0) is completely arbitrary. It could be any intersection in the city. This is an example of the arbitrariness in the choice of 'zero' discussed above.

Another major contribution of Descartes—one that we will use implicitly in later chapters—was the development of the field known as analytic geometry, which basically brings together algebra and geometry.

Here's a simple example of analytic geometry in action: consider the equation

$$y = x^2$$

We can interpret this algebraic equation as a set of instructions for finding points in a Cartesian grid. If we move one unit to the right on the x axis, then $y = 1$, which means that we should move up one unit of the y axis. Similarly, if you go two units to the right on the x axis you will go four units up on the y axis, while three units on the x axis corresponds to nine units on the y axis and so on. The equation, in other words, can be converted into a line on a graph—a line that, in this case, is a steeply rising curve known as a parabola.

The point of this little exercise is to show the close relationship between algebraic equations and geometrical curves. One result of this duality is that it is possible to solve algebraic problems by using geometry and geometrical problems by using algebra. Another important result historically was that the duality is also a crucial element in the development of calculus.

Having gone through the development of coordinate systems and Euclidean geometry, we will close this chapter by returning to a point that was made earlier—the fact that throughout history it was assumed (usually unconsciously) that Euclidean geometry was the only possible geometrical system. This assumption is understandable. The world we experience every day does appear to be a flat plane, and the Euclidean theorems seem to apply.

Yet we only have to go back to the latitude-longitude-altitude example with which we started this chapter to realize that we do not really live in a Euclidean world. To see this, picture a triangle, two of whose sides are meridians of longitude, with the third side being a segment of the equator. The meridians meet the equator to form right angles, which means that the sum of the angles at the base of our triangle is 180 degrees. But there is a third angle—the one at the pole. Consequently, the angles in this triangle add up to more than 180 degrees, in contradiction to the theorem we proved above.

The only way to deal with this fact is to say that the geometry on the surface of a sphere is not governed by Euclid's axioms. It is the simplest example of what is called non-Euclidean geometry. There are many such geometries—the surface of a saddle is another common example. In the nineteenth century, a number of mathematicians, most notably Bernhard Riemann (1826–1866) in Germany, began to explore other kinds of geometry, including systems well beyond these simplest examples. As we shall see in Chapter 11, what is called Riemannian geometry was a tool that Einstein needed to develop general relativity. In essence, Riemann realized that to describe a general geometry, you had to add more coordinates to the ones we have been considering so far. These new coordinates describe the curvature of space at each point. (For the expert, I note that this requires the use of a mathematical construct called a tensor.)

It's important to realize that the development of non-Euclidean geometries has nothing to do with the question of whether or not Euclidean geometry describes the real world. From the time of Eratosthenes, scholars had known that the Earth was a sphere—in fact, Eratosthenes made a reasonable measurement of its radius. Greek mathematicians proved many theorems about three-dimensional figures like spheres and cones. Modern surveyors know that they may have to correct their measurements for the curvature of the Earth. Nevertheless, it wasn't until the nineteenth century that serious thought was given to the issue on non-Euclidean systems.

With this introduction to the notion of coordinate systems, then, we are ready to move on to the foundations of relativity.

4

FOUNDATIONS OF SPECIAL RELATIVITY

EINSTEIN'S *RELATIVITY* CHAPTERS 4–7

Things are seldom what they seem.
W.S. Gilbert and Arthur Sullivan, *HMS Pinafore*

In these chapters Einstein starts laying the groundwork for the special theory of relativity. He introduces the idea that if the Newtonian approach to the addition of velocities is true, then a problem arises when we consider the speed of electromagnetic radiation. He concludes that we will have to examine the concept of time more carefully.

We can start our discussion of relativity by introducing the concept of the frame of reference, which is nothing more than the place from which an observer looks at the universe. For example, right now you are sitting in a frame of reference attached to the Earth. You can, if you like, imagine yourself to be at the (0, 0, 0) point in a Cartesian coordinate system that stretches away from you in all directions.

Someone going by in a car is also in a frame of reference, but it's not the same as yours since it's moving with respect to you. Everybody is in some frame of reference, and relativity is the branch of science that tells us how to relate measurements made by observers in different frames.

We can make several points about frames of reference. First, every observer feels that he or she is stationary in his or her own frame. To you, that person in the car is moving past you at a certain speed—let's say at 20 mph toward the east. The person in the car, however, would say that he or she is stationary and that you are moving at 20 mph toward the west. As we shall see in more detail later, observers in different frames of reference will generally give different descriptions of events.

Because all of us have lived our lives in the Earth's surface, there is a natural tendency to think of a reference frame fixed to the Earth as somehow 'right'. But think about that for a moment. Your 'fixed' frame rotates with the Earth, which means that you have traveled hundreds of miles in the last hour without being aware of it. Furthermore, the Earth is revolving around the sun, which means that you've also traveled thousands of miles around the Earth's orbit in that same hour. Add in the fact that the sun revolves around the center of the Milky Way galaxy every 250 million years or so and the fact that the Milky Way is participating in the general expansion of the universe and you can see that there is nothing 'fixed' about your Earth-bound frame of reference.

In the Newtonian picture there is an implicit assumption that there is a 'right' frame of reference from which to view the world. It's generally called the 'God's eye view' these days, a designation that would fit with the religious orientation of Newton's time. You can think of relativity as a successful attempt by Einstein to remove that assumption from physics and to argue that all frames of reference are equally valid.

We need to introduce one more important term before we move on to the development of relativity. In the example of the car given above, the two frames of reference are moving with a constant velocity. Such frames are said to be *inertial*. This distinguishes them from frames that might be accelerating or rotating with respect to each other. It turns out to be much easier to deal with inertial frames, and it is to them that we will first turn our attention.

Now let's imagine a simple experiment. As your friend goes by in a car, he or she throws a ball straight up into the air and catches it when it falls. How do you and the moving observer describe what you see?

The observer in the car sees the ball go straight up and fall straight back down. You, on the other hand, see the ball move along with the car as it ascends and continue to move laterally as it falls. In other words, you see the ball follow a curved path (a path known, incidentally, as a parabola).

Once again, two different observers give different descriptions of an event. It's obvious in this example that neither observer is 'right'. Both descriptions are correct in the frame of reference in which they are given.

But what if we ask a different question of our observers? What if, instead of asking them to describe the event, we ask them to describe the laws of nature that govern the event? Suppose further that we equip each observer with a fully fledged physics laboratory and all the assistants and funding the heart could desire. What laws would they discover?

This is the key point in the formulation of relativity, because according to Newton's Laws of Motion (see Chapter 2), the two observers would come up with exactly the same laws of mechanics. We can call this the principle of Newtonian relativity:

> The laws of mechanics are the same in all inertial frames of reference.

Thus, although different observers give different descriptions of events, they agree on the basic laws of mechanics that give rise to those events. We can extend this idea to other areas of classical physics by saying:

> The laws of nature are the same in all inertial frames of reference.

This is called the Principle of Special Relativity, and it will give rise, as we shall see, to the theory of special relativity. The 'special' arises because this principle is restricted to inertial frames of reference. Special relativity is a relatively simple theory and was the subject of Einstein's famous 1905 paper. If we relax the requirement of non-accelerated motion we can make a statement like:

> The laws of nature are the same in all frames of reference, accelerated or not.

This is called the Principle of General Relativity and gives rise to the general theory of relativity. This theory involves, as we shall see in Chapter 9, a much more difficult mathematical formulation, a statement that is attested to by the fact that it took a man of Einstein's genius over a decade to work it out.

The Principle of Special Relativity is built into mechanics which, as we saw in Chapter 2, is one of the pillars of the classical scientific world view.

Unfortunately, as we shall see shortly, the Principle seems to come into conflict with another of those pillars—the science of electromagnetism.

We can see how this conflict is generated by going back to our observers in two inertial frame of reference. Suppose the observer in the moving car throws a ball forward. In his or her frame of reference, let's suppose the ball is traveling at a speed of 40 miles per hour. How fast will it be traveling as far as the observer on the ground is concerned?

Our first reaction is to say 60 miles per hour—40 for the ball plus 20 for the motion of the car. This, in fact, is the Newtonian result, and it seems quite reasonable, quite in line with our intuition. But let's look at it in a little more detail and see if we can't uncover some unspoken assumptions in our reasoning.

Speed is defined to be the distance an object travels divided by the time it takes to cover that distance. The observer in the car would, therefore, have to have a yardstick to measure distance and a stopwatch to measure the time of flight of the ball. He or she might, for example, use a stopwatch to see where the ball was after one second, then use the yardstick to measure how far the ball had traveled.

The observer on the ground would presumably go through the same procedure using his or her own clock and yardstick. And here is where the unspoken assumption comes in, because to get the Newtonian result, you have to assume that the two clocks—one in the frame of each observer—keep time at the same rate, and that the two yardsticks measure the same distances. In the Newtonian world, the correct time is kept by a clock in the 'God's eye' frame of reference and all other clocks are synchronized to it, so this assumption is justified. I bring this up because if there is no God's eye frame, we can no longer make this assumption and we might have to re-think our ideas about space (i.e. distance) and time.

Now let's imagine a different experiment. Suppose that instead of throwing a ball, your friend in the car shines a flashlight. How fast will that beam of light be traveling in the two frames of reference?

In Chapter 2 we saw that electromagnetic waves like light travel through empty space at the speed we denote by the letter 'c', 186,000 miles per second. Clearly, the person in the car who is holding the flashlight will see the light traveling with this speed in his or her frame of reference. The interesting question is what you see standing on the ground.

If we follow the same reasoning as we did for the ball, we would have to say that an observer on the ground would see the light moving with a speed c plus the speed of the car. But this creates a problem, because as we saw in Chapter 2, the speed of light is built into Maxwell's equations, so this result would mean that Maxwell's equations would be different in the two frames of reference. This, of course, would violate the Principle of Relativity.

There are three ways around this dilemma:

- The Principle of Relativity could be wrong.
- Maxwell's equations could be wrong.
- Our unspoken assumptions about time and distance could be wrong.

Let's look at these options one at a time. As we mentioned above, the Principle of Relativity follows from Newton's Laws of Motion. This does not guarantee that it has to apply to other areas of science. It is, however, such a beautiful and compelling idea that abandoning it should be seen as a last resort—something we will do only if the data forces us to.

Maxwell's equations certainly matched experiments available to scientists at the end of the nineteenth century. Some people wondered, however, if there weren't terms missing from the equations—terms that would make the speed of electromagnetic radiation depend on the motion of the source. After all, 'c' is such a large number that it might very well obscure a term that depended on the relatively tiny speeds of ordinary material objects.

Finally, we note that if it turns out that the third option is the one we want to pursue, then the simple addition of velocities that worked for the baseball is going to be modified. We will return to this point in Chapters 6 and 7.

In any case, there is only one way to decide which of these three options will get us out of our dilemma, and that is to see which of them gives results that agree with experiment. Here's an example of how such a testing procedure might occur.

Let's look at the second option above and assume that Maxwell's equations really do contain a hitherto unknown term making the speed of light dependent on the speed of the source. If there is such a term, then the light emitted by a source moving toward you will be traveling faster than the light emitted by the same source when it is moving away from you.

As it happens, there are systems in nature that make it possible to test this prediction. Most of the stars we see in the sky are not single objects, but multiple star systems. In a double star system, for example, two stars revolve around each other in times that can be as short as days or weeks. Imagine that such a system is aligned so that the plane of the orbit, when extended, passes through the Earth. In this case, a star will appear to be moving straight toward us at one point in its orbit and straight away from us half a period later. Using standard optical techniques, astronomers can look for changes in the light emitted at these two points in the star's orbit. When they do so, they see no difference in the speed of that light. In this case, the observation clearly rules out the possibility of extra terms in Maxwell's equation.

But by far the most interesting attempt to reconcile Newton and Maxwell involved the concept of the luminiferous ether. You will recall from Chapter 2 that the prediction of the existence of electromagnetic waves led naturally to the question of the identity of the medium on which the waves moved. The preferred answer in the late nineteenth century was that these waves moved on a medium called the ether.

This is actually an old idea, going back to Aristotle's famous dictum that 'Nature abhors a vacuum'. The basic idea is that the universe is filled with this tenuous stuff, and electromagnetic waves move on the ether much as ripples move across water or sound moves through the air. During the late nineteenth century physicists took this idea very seriously, producing complex models for the ether full of gears and sprockets and other mechanical devices.

The existence of an ether would get us out of the dilemma posed above, because if there was an ether, it would define the 'God's eye' frame of reference we talked about above. The idea is that you would say that the laws of nature are correct in the rest frame of the ether but had to be modified if they are described in other frames. In essence, this was an attempt to exercise the first option given above—to get rid of the Principle of Relativity.

There was, however, a major impediment to this approach, one that Kelvin pointed out in his 'dark cloud' speech. This was, of course, the Michelson–Morley experiment. There are actually two interesting questions to ask about this experiment. One concerns the attempts by scientists to rescue the concept of the ether from the results. The other concerns the question of whether, despite the historical importance of this experiment in retrospect, it actually had any influence on the young Albert Einstein when he was developing the theory of relativity.

We can begin by describing the experiment in a little more detail. Here's an analogy that may help. Imagine that you have two rowboats that move at the same speed on still water. Suppose we take these rowboats to a wide river and assign them two different tasks. One is told to row downstream (i.e. with the current) for a certain distance, then turn around and row against the current back to the starting point. The other boat is to row across the river to a spot opposite the starting point and then return. Finally, suppose that we adjust the distance so that if there were no current the boats would arrive back at the starting point at the same time.

Working out the return times of the rowboats is a standard problem in freshman physics courses. If there is a current, the boats will not, in general, return at the same time. (You can get some sense of how this might be so by noting that one boat will go downstream very quickly since it is moving with the current but take much longer to get back against the current.)

Now substitute two light beams that start out perfectly aligned (i.e. crest to crest, trough to trough) for the rowboats and the ether wind caused by the Earth's motion for the river current. This, in essence, is the Michelson–Morley experiment, with the light beams being turned around by mirrors. The fact that the two light beams leave perfectly aligned and are no longer aligned on their return gives rise to a phenomenon known as interference which, in this experiment, manifests itself as the production of a series of light and dark rings on a detector or photographic plate.

The key point of the experiment is not that we see rings—small errors in the placement of the mirrors would produce the same effect. The key point is that the rings you see do not change over the course of a year. The Earth's motion around the sun would have the effect of reversing the direction of the ether wind every six months—in effect, reversing the direction of the river in our example. It was this lack of change that Kelvin called a 'dark cloud'.

Experiments like this are very difficult to do. The main problem faced by the scientists is making sure that they are seeing real effects, effects that are not produced by vibrations in the environment. Michelson and Morley, for example, floated their apparatus on a pool of mercury contained in a concrete pillar in the basement of their building. Today, scientists doing these kinds of delicate experiments not only have to worry about vibrations caused by things like passing cars, but even the effect of wind blowing on their building.

Nevertheless, as we saw in Chapter 2, the results of this experiment were unambiguous. There was no evidence for an ether wind. How could we reconcile this result with the existence of the ether?

The first attempt was straightforward. What if, people argued, the ether in the vicinity of the Earth was carried along with the planet, more or less like a second atmosphere? In this case there would be no ether wind associated with the Earth's orbital motion, just as there is no movement of the air due to the same motion.

Unfortunately, there is a well-known astronomical effect called stellar aberration that tells us that this can't be the answer. Stellar aberration is a change in the apparent position of a star because of the motion of the Earth, and had been observed since the eighteenth century. Here's a simple analogy to explain how it works. Imagine that you are standing in the rain. There is no wind, so the drops fall straight down and you hold your umbrella straight up to keep dry. Now imagine that you start walking—in essence, that you move from your stationary frame of reference to a moving one. In your new frame of reference you will have to tilt your umbrella forward because it will appear to you that the rain is coming in at an angle. Substitute rays of light from a distant star for the raindrops in this analogy and you have stellar aberration.

The attempt to rescue the ether hypothesis by saying that the ether moves along with the Earth would be equivalent to assuming that the atmosphere was moving along with you in our raindrop analogy. If this happened, of course, the raindrops would always fall straight down and you would never have to tilt your umbrella. In the same way, if ether moved along with the Earth there would be no stellar aberration—no change in the angle of sight to a star due to the Earth's motion.

But there is such a change. It was first discovered accidentally by astronomers seeking to prove the Copernican hypothesis that the Earth moves around the sun rather than vice versa. It had been known for over a century before Michelson and Morley began their experiment.

Before moving on, we should point out that stellar aberration is not the same as a somewhat similar astronomical effect known as stellar parallax. The latter is the apparent shift in position of a star against the stellar background when the star is observed from two separate positions. This was first seen in the early nineteenth century and is an important technique used in establishing the distance to nearby stars.

The list of people who wrestled with the problem of the ether in the latter part of the nineteenth century reads like a *Who's Who* of science. We will mention just one such attempt because it anticipated the results of special relativity. The Dutch physicist Hendrik Lorentz (1853–1928) pointed out that the Michelson–Morley result could be understood if objects moving through the ether had their length shortened by an amount $\sqrt{1-\left(\dfrac{v}{c}\right)^2}$. As we shall see later, this so-called Lorentz contraction follows from the hypotheses of special relativity. When Lorentz first proposed it, however, it was based on the idea that it was motion through the ether that produced the contraction.

So there you have it. Returning to the three options listed above, we see that there is no experimental reason to modify Maxwell's equations to include modifications of the speed of light due to the motion of the source. We also see that the most obvious 'God's eye' frame of reference— the rest frame of the ether—is in serious trouble, since the combination of the Michelson–Morley experiment and stellar aberration seems to lead to the conclusion that the ether simply doesn't exist. This leaves us with our third option, a close examination of our notions of space and time. This, of course, was the path taken by Albert Einstein in the Swiss patent office.

Before turning to the development of special relativity we should take a few moments to examine a mild scholarly controversy about the role that the Michelson–Morley experiment played in Einstein's thinking in 1905. Because the experiment seems so important to us in retrospect, there has grown up what historian Gerald Holton calls a 'legend' that it played an important role in Einstein's thinking. The experiment certainly makes a convenient point from which to launch into a pedagogical treatment of relativity, so one's first expectation is that it must have been that way for Einstein as well.

The first hint that things might not be so straightforward comes from the fact that Einstein neither mentioned nor referenced the Michelson–Morley work in his 1905 paper. A word of explanation: it was (and remains) a major obligation of every scholar writing a paper to credit the work of others that have contributed to the new results. It's hard to imagine that Einstein would have neglected to carry out this basic obligation, especially since a well-filled-out set of references was (and is) considered to be the hallmark of a competent scholar.

Holton's article in the journal *Isis* (vol. 60, 1969, pp.132–197) traces out the attempts of scholars to answer the question of how much the Michelson–Morley experiment influenced Einstein's early work. The main problem is that there are no contemporary documents—documents that might have told us what Einstein was thinking at the time. Consequently, we have to depend on material collected by historians that come from later in Einstein's life. In some cases, a gap of almost 50 years between the events and their recollection raises questions about their accuracy, of course.

For example, here's a statement from a letter Einstein wrote to a colleague in 1954:

> In my own development Michelson's result has not had a considerable influence. I even do not remember if I knew of it at all when I wrote my first paper on the subject (in 1905).

Or from a 1952 letter:

> The influence of the famous Michelson–Morley experiment on my own deliberations has been rather indirect.

These sorts of statements (and there are many like them in letters he wrote in the 1950s) would seem to settle the issue. If he said that the experiment didn't have much of an effect, then it couldn't have had much of an effect.

But there is another source of information, more indirect, but closer in time to the original work. We mentioned in Chapter 1 that Einstein made a trip to Japan in 1922. In fact, he was in Japan from November 17 to December 29 of that year, a guest of the publisher Kaizo-Sha. During this visit he gave a talk to physics students at Kyoto University on what was described as a 'cold, snowy day'. His translator for the visit was a young Japanese physicist named Jun Ishiwara, a man who had studied in Munich for two years before World War I and who would later translate Einstein's works into Japanese. From these facts we can deduce that Ishiwara had a good command of German. According to an article that appeared in *Historical Studies in the Physical and Biological Sciences* (vol. 31, 2000, pp.1–35), Ishiwara's notes on that lecture had Einstein saying the following:

> When I had these idea in mind as a student, I came to know the strange result of Michelson's experiment...This was the first route that led me to what we now call the Principle of Special Relativity.

What are we to make of this kind of historical data? Do we trust Einstein's recollections fifty years after the fact and assume that there was some sort of flaw in the trail of information from 1922 lecture to notes to translation to publication? Or do we trust the translation and assign Einstein's later statements to a failure of memory?

This is a question on which reasonable people can (and do) differ. My own tendency is to assign great weight to the fact that Einstein didn't reference the Michelson–Morley paper and trust his later statements.

In any case, with this introduction Einstein begins to think about the nature of time and space and to develop the special theory of relativity.

5

TIME

EINSTEIN'S *RELATIVITY* CHAPTER 8

What then is time? If no one asks me, I know what it is. If I wish to explain it to him who asks, I do not know.

Saint Augustine

The Khazars believe that at the bottom of the Caspian Sea there is a blind fish that keeps time for the entire world.

Milorad Pavič, *The Dictionary of the Khazars* (female edition)

In this chapter Einstein begins to take on the difficult subject of defining time. His basic approach is to start with the concept of simultaneity and move on to the question of whether or not two identical clocks will run at the same rate when they are separated.

Physicists do not attempt to define what time is, but only to find ways to measure it. As Saint Augustine pointed out, trying to define the nature of time is a hopeless philosophical venture. Instead, what physicists do is to find a regularly repeating event and then measure all other time intervals in terms of the number of repetitions of that event that occur during the interval. You can get a rough notion of this process by imagining a grandfather clock with a pendulum swinging away. Suppose you define the time it takes for the pendulum to swing from one side to the other to be one second. Then you would determine the number of seconds it took for anything else to happen—the time it took a dropped ball to hit the ground, for example—by counting the number of times the pendulum was able to swing during that event.

There is a long history of human attempts to measure time. There are, in fact, three naturally occurring 'clocks' readily available to us. One is the rotation of the Earth on its axis, which defines the unit of time we call the 'day'. Then there is the revolution of the Earth around the sun, which defines the unit of time we call the 'year'. Finally, there are the changing phases of the moon, which define the unit of time called the 'lunar month' (about 28 days).

Of these time intervals, the year was arguably the most important for early agricultural societies. In modern language, it is the position of the Earth in its orbit that determines where we are in the seasonal cycle, and hence when to plant crops and carry out other activities. The most obvious way to determine when one year ends and another begins is to pick an event such as the solstice and start counting days. You might, for example, know that a certain number of days into the count you should plant peas and potatoes, at a different number of days it was time to plant corn, and so on. In point of fact, you would be constructing a calendar, the most primitive device for measuring time.

As we shall see in a moment, the modern calendar was developed over millennia. It is easy for us to take it for granted, but we have to keep in mind that for most of recorded history it did not exist.

The basic problem in constructing a calendar is that there are not an even number of days in a year. In modern terms (i.e. terms that would not have been used by the ancients) if we started counting sunrises when the Earth was at a particular point in its orbit, when we got to 365 the Earth would not be at the same place where it started. It would, in fact, be about 6 hours away from that place. After four circuits it would be a full day behind. It's not hard to see that if you didn't take this slippage into account, eventually you would be celebrating Christmas in the middle of summer.

One of the great surprises in the late twentieth century was the realization that very primitive societies all around the world had come to terms with this problem. Perhaps the best embodiment of this knowledge is Stonehenge, that great assembly of stones sitting on Salisbury Plain in southern England. Despite its current association with modern Druids, the monument was actually thousands of years old by the time the Druids came around. The earliest part of the monument was built about 5000 years ago by people who had neither writing nor metal tools. In terms of our discussion, the most important property of Stonehenge is that on the day of the summer solstice—the longest day of the year—a person standing in the center of the stone rings sees the sun come up over an upright stone a little less than a hundred yards away. Sunrise over this so-called Heel Stone, then, is an event that fixes the position of the Earth in its orbit around the sun, and hence provides a starting point for counting the days in the new year. That such a monument could have been built by people with such a low level of technology is a testament to human ingenuity. It is also a testament to the fact that the universe is regular and predictable, a statement which is, of course, the foundation of all science.

We can think of Stonehenge, then, as a kind of calendar, a device for dealing with the fact that there are not an even number of days in a year. The fact that it served as a calendar, however, does not mean that it was only a calendar. Stonehenge, in fact, sits in the middle of one of the largest collections of Neolithic structures in the world. There are other monuments and many barrow graves, which leads modern scholars to suggest that the area had particular religious significance for these people. Some scholars have also suggested that it may have been seen as a place of healing, something like modern day Lourdes.

But whatever Stonehenge's place in the societies it served, the discovery of its astronomical function triggered an entirely new area of science called archeoastronomy. It was found that many ancient monuments, both in Europe and the Americas, marked significant events in the sky. One particularly interesting example are the so-called medicine wheels in the American and Canadian west. These aren't particularly imposing structures—they are basically just rocks laid in a pattern on the ground. The point, though, is that someone sitting in a designated spot and looking along the spokes of the wheel will see something analogous to the sun coming up over the Heel Stone. What is surprising about the medicine wheels, though, is that they were built by nomadic hunters, not by farmers. Keeping the seasons straight is obviously not purely an agricultural concern.

In any case, as civilizations developed, they each found their own way of dealing with time. My personal favorite scheme was that of the ancient Egyptians, who had twelve months of thirty days each day year followed by a five-day festival/party. (Some scholars trace our own New Year's celebration back to this Egyptian source.) This calendar would suffer from the slippage we discussed above, of course. In 123 BC the rulers of Alexandria issued an edict that would, in effect, insert an extra day every four years to keep the calendar in line with the seasons, but it wasn't widely enforced or observed.

So long as the various societies were largely isolated from each other, the proliferation of and differences between calendars caused no problems. By the first century BC, however, the Roman Empire was in the process of incorporating the entire Mediterranean basin into a single political entity, and it was time to produce a single universal calendar. One of the things that Julius Caesar did was to appoint a commission to produce a uniform calendar. This so-called Julian calendar is quite similar to the one we use today, with an extra day added every four years to deal with the slippage problem outlined above. Unlike his Alexandrian predecessors, Caesar had the means of imposing his new calendar. (We still honor the man for this accomplishment—the month of July is named for him.) To get things straightened out when the new calendar was introduced, Caesar inserted two extra months plus twenty-three extra days in 46 BC, making it the longest year on record.

Unfortunately, the year is not exactly 365¼ days long—it's actually eleven minutes, fourteen seconds shorter than this. Thus, as much as the Julian calendar was an improvement over the Egyptian calendar, it, too, would gradually accumulate errors. By 1545, for example, astronomical events used to set the date for Easter had drifted a full ten days. Consequently, in 1582 Pope Gregory XIII promulgated a new calendar, the one we use today. The main difference from the Julian calendar is that there are leap years only every fourth centennial year, so that while 2000 was a leap year, 1700, 1800, and 1900 were not. To get the new system started, the Pope decreed that in 1582 the day after October 5 would be October 15, making that the shortest year on record.

The adoption of the Gregorian calendar did not always go smoothly. When England switched over in 1754, for example, there is a legend (probably apocryphal) that there were riots by people demanding that their 'lost days' be returned. The Russian Czars never adopted the calendar at all, but retained the Julian. Because of this, there remains some confusion about whether the Russian Revolution actually happened in October or November. Nevertheless, the Gregorian calendar is used throughout the world today.

Turning our attention to defining shorter time periods, we note that the Egyptians were the first to subdivide the day. They defined the hour as one twelfth of the time between sunrise and sunset—a definition under which the length of the hour not only varied with the seasons, but which left no 'hour' at night. The development of mechanical clocks in medieval Europe appears to have been driven by the need of monastic orders to maintain the schedule of their devotional activities, but by the beginnings of the modern era, most towns had at least one mechanical clock.

Eventually, a standard second was defined to be 1/86,400 the length of the mean solar day. Thus, the second was simply a fraction of one of the three basic clocks we discussed above—the one tied to the Earth's rotation.

By the end of the nineteenth century, however, an unexpected problem developed. During that century, high tech pendulum clocks (think of them as sophisticated grandfather clocks) kept getting more and more accurate. Eventually they became accurate enough so that various physical effects that change the length of the day could start to demand attention.

There are a number of such effects. One is the action of the tides, which slows down the Earth's daily rotation by a few milliseconds per century. We know from fossil corals that four hundred million years ago the day was about three hours shorter than it is now, for example, and theorists suggest that when the Earth was first formed the day may have been as short as six hours. Other effects, like the precession of the Earth's axis of rotation, produce even larger effects than the tides. Finally, things like the blowing of the wind or the redistribution of mass following a major earthquake can affect the length of the day if you have an accurate enough clock. All of these effects combine to produce both predictable and erratic changes in the length of the day. Clearly, the Earth's rotation was not going to be a reliable time standard in the twentieth century.

In 1956 the International Committee on Weights and Measures, which is in charge of such things, redefined the second to be 1/31,566,935.9747 of the length of the year 1900. In effect, they replaced the rotation of the Earth on its axis by the revolution of the Earth in its orbit as their basic timekeeper. This solved the problem of the erratic rotation, but it's not a terribly convenient standard. Ideally, you would want a standard that people could reproduce in their own laboratories.

Enter the atomic clock. From the 1950s on, scientists began looking to events inside the atom for their basic time interval, instead of the motion of the Earth. No winds blow on the electron, and there are no tides, so atomic standards promise to bypass some of the problems we've been discussing. Let's take a few moments to discuss how the atom can be used to define time.

The standard picture of the atom has negatively charged electrons circling the positively charged nucleus. Less well known, perhaps, is the fact that in general both the nucleus and the electrons can be thought of as tiny magnets. This effect arises from the fact that both the electron and the nucleus are spinning on their axes, like miniature planets. The electron and nuclear magnets interact with each other, as magnets do, and the energy locked up in the mutually created magnetic field is slightly different when the north poles of both magnets are pointing in the same direction as it is when they are pointing in opposite directions. Since the direction of a particle's magnet depends on how the particle is spinning— i.e. on whether it is spinning clockwise or counterclockwise—this energy difference is ultimately related to the particle's rate of rotation. In effect, the spinning electron can be used to replace the spinning Earth as a time standard.

For technical reasons, the element cesium, a soft, silvery metal, was used in the first atomic clocks. The design of the clock is simple to describe, if not simple to realize in the laboratory. Cesium is vaporized in a small furnace and the atoms are brought out into a beam line. There external magnets split the beam into two components: one with the north pole of the electron's magnet pointing up, the other with it pointing down. The forces exerted by the external magnets send these two components in different directions (they actually go off down different beam pipes).

At this point the beam in which the electrons have their north pole pointing down enters a chamber filled with microwave radiation. If this radiation has the right frequency, it can flip the electron's magnet so that the north pole is pointing up. The beam then leaves the chamber and encounters a second set of external magnets, and the electrons whose north pole is pointing up (i.e. the electrons that were flipped in the radiation chamber) are counted. The frequency of the microwave radiation that produces the maximum number of electrons entering the counter is noted, because the energy of that radiation is precisely the energy between the two possible states of the electron (north pole up and north pole down).

In 1964 the International Commission on Weights and Measures adopted an alternative standard for the definition of the second, saying that a second was the time it took the microwave radiation in a cesium atomic clock to reverse itself 9,192,631,770 times. For a few years both this and the definition in terms of the year 1900 were in place, but by 1967 the technology of atomic clocks had advanced to the point that they became the sole definition and the year 1900 definition was dropped.

Since the 1950s, a lot of bells and whistles have been added to the basic design outlined above. For example, other atoms such as rubidium have replaced the cesium in some clocks, and so-called 'fountain' designs, in which the beam of atoms is run through the radiation chamber twice, have achieved incredible accuracies. In 2011 a cesium fountain clock in England reported an accuracy of 16 decimal places. A clock that accurate could be expected to gain or lose no more than a second if it ran for 138 million years! (For reference, some of the early 1950s atomic clocks would lose a second in 'only' three hundred years.)

We note in passing that this progression in defining basic standards can be seen in areas beyond timekeeping. The goal of the scientists involved in this kind of work is to develop a standard that could be duplicated in every laboratory on the planet. In the example we've just been discussing, for example, these efforts have reached the point where any group that can afford an atomic clock can maintain its own time standard. In a similar way, we will see in Chapter 6 that the meter, which used to be defined as the distance between two scratches on a platinum-iridium bar kept in a vault near Paris, is now defined as the distance light travels in a certain fraction of a second. Again, this is a standard that can be reproduced in the laboratory. The only 'old-fashioned' fundamental standard left is the kilogram, which is defined in terms of the mass of a platinum-iridium block in that same vault, and many scientists are trying to develop a modern mass standard to replace it.

The result of all this is that today the world operates on two separate time standards. So-called Universal Time (UT) is geared to the length of the day as measured at the Royal Observatory in Greenwich, London. You can think of this as the time between situations where the sun crosses the meridian at Greenwich. For technical reasons, this time is now measured by looking at distant quasars with sophisticated radio telescopes instead of at the sun. Basically, what you do is start a clock when the quasar crosses the meridian on one day, and stop the counting when it crosses the meridian on the next day. You should recognize UT (which used to be called Greenwich Mean Time) as our old friend, the use of the rotation of the Earth as our basic timekeeper.

The second time system is based on atomic clocks, and is called TA1 (for *Temps Atomique 1*). It is kept by a network of atomic clocks around the world. At the levels of accuracy these clocks can achieve, it is not always easy to compare their results. To give one example of why this should be so, we shall see in Chapter 9 that the effects of General Relativity will alter (very slightly) the operation of clocks at different altitudes because the clocks are in slightly different gravitational fields. Thus, TA1 time is generally determined by combining the measurements of all the clocks in the network, rather than by reference to any single clock.

By now you will realize that UT and TA1 are actually measuring time using different standards—the rotation of the Earth (UT) and the rotation of the electron (TA1). As we saw above, the rotation of the Earth varies over time, so the times displayed on these two clocks would gradually diverge from one another if nothing is done to prevent this from happening. To keep the atom and the Earth synchronized, since the 1970s scientists have occasionally inserted 'leap seconds' into the year. This happens when the atomic clocks 'vote' that the time measured by the two standards has diverged by 0.9 seconds. At a second before midnight on June 30, 2012, for example, an extra second was added to TA1 to restore the agreement between the two clocks. Thus are the Earth and the electron reconciled.

This process has given rise to a minor conflict in the scientific community. Astronomers, of course, want to keep the appearance of the sky in tune with atomic clocks, so they generally support the insertion of the leap second. Computer people, however, argue that this makes their job more difficult, since they have to adjust the internal clocks in their machines. There have been so far about 25 leap seconds, inserted at irregular times since the 1970s. The real problem, though, is that it is not possible to predict when the next leap second will be needed (remember what we said about earthquakes above), which introduces an unwelcome complication into the world of computers. So far the astronomers seem to be winning this debate.

With this understanding of what it means to measure time, we can move on to see how special relativity changes our idea of time's properties.

6

SPECIAL RELATIVITY
EINSTEIN'S *RELATIVITY* CHAPTERS 9–14

There was a young lady named Bright
Who could travel much faster than light.
She set out one day
In a relative way
And returned on the previous night.

Traditional limerick

In these chapters, Einstein works out the quantitative predictions of special relativity. He begins with the concept of simultaneity discussed in the last chapter, then moves on to examine the consequences of relativity for moving clocks and meter sticks. Finally, he derives the relativistic equation for the addition of velocities and shows that the speed of light can, indeed, be the same in all inertial frames of reference.

With his preliminary discussion of coordinate systems, time, and the principle of special relativity out of the way, Einstein is ready to begin developing his theory. He begins with what appears to be the simplest possible concept, the notion of simultaneity. Two events are said to be simultaneous if they happen at the same time. In the Newtonian world, events that are simultaneous in one frame of reference are simultaneous in all frames, since all events are referred to a universal time. Whether this is true in a world where we are re-examining our notions of space and time, however, remains to be seen.

Let's follow Einstein and look at a situation where two lightning strokes hit a railroad track at two different places. Under what circumstances will these two events, separated by some distance, be simultaneous?

To make the situation clear, let's start in a frame fixed to the Earth and assume that there is an observer standing at each of the points hit by lightning and another observer midway between the two points. When the lightning hits, each observer at a point of impact sends a light signal toward the one in the middle. In this situation, it is obvious that the two signals will arrive at the position of the central observer at the same time—after all, they are both traveling the same distance. Thus, the central observer will say that the two lightning strikes are simultaneous in his frame of reference. That observer would say the same thing if a different signal, such as sound, were used.

Now let's ask how the same sequence of events will be recorded by an observer on a railroad car moving to the east at a constant velocity when the lightning bolts strike. This observer will, of course, perceive himself or herself to be at rest, and will note the three observers on the ground moving by to the west. How will the lightning strikes we've just described be recorded by the observer on the train?

That observer will be moving toward the lightning bolt on the right and away from the lightning bolt on the left. The observer on the train will be moving toward the ground observer on the right and away from the ground observer on the left. This means that as the signals from the ground observers move toward the central observer, the moving observer will be moving to meet one signal and moving away from another. Thus, the bolt on the right will be observed to strike first, and the bolt on the left will be observed to strike later.

As a result of these considerations, we can say that:

> Events that are simultaneous in one frame of reference are not necessarily simultaneous in another.

Having said this, we need to note that the loss of simultaneity depends on the fact that the two events being observed are separated in space. If you go through the argument above, you will realize that both observers will observe the events as simultaneous if the events take place at the same point in space.

It's important to remember what we are doing here. In Chapter 3 we pointed out that one way of resolving the apparent contradiction between the principle of relativity and electromagnetism was to re-examine our notions of space and time. The re-consideration of the concept of simultaneity is our first step in this re-examination. The crucial point, however, is that we will only know if this is the right way to proceed when our re-examination produces predictions that can be compared with experimental results. We will examine the experimental evidence for both special and general relativity in later chapters, but at this point in our development we are simply in the process of determining where this line of inquiry leads us.

The fact that a concept as simple as simultaneity depends on one's frame of reference should suggest to us that time itself might also be frame dependent. To see whether this is so, let us define a simple clock in this way: there is a flashbulb that goes off, sending a beam of light up to a mirror located a distance D away. The light is reflected back down and is detected by a phototube next to the flashbulb. As soon as the phototube is activated a signal is sent to the flashbulb and the entire process is repeated. The operation of this 'light clock' is a regularly repeating phenomenon of the type we discussed in Chapter 5, a process that can be used to define a time standard.

Because the concept of the light clock may seem a bit contrived, I would like to take a moment to discuss the role of hypothetical experiments in Einstein's presentation of relativity (and, for that matter, in the Bohr–Einstein debates discussed in Chapter 1). This type of experiment, which is imagined but not actually done, is called a *gedanken* experiment (from the German *denken*, to think). Its purpose is to show, in as simple and straightforward a way as possible, how a particular principle works. It is, for example, extremely unlikely that anyone would actually build the kind of light clock described above. Nevertheless, the clock provides a simple way to illustrate some important points about relativity, as we shall see.

It's important to realize that although the light clock may seem a bit contrived, it is nonetheless a perfectly good clock with which to investigate the properties of time. To see this, you need only realize that we can adjust the 'tick' of the time clock by varying the distance D between the flashbulb and the mirror. Imagine, for example, that you had a grandfather clock sitting next to a light clock. You could adjust D so that the light clock flashed every time the pendulum reached its maximum angle. In this case the light clock and the grandfather clock would be synchronized and anything we learn about time by doing *gedanken* experiments with the light clock would have to be true of the grandfather clock as well.

Pick any clock you want and a simple adjustment of D will synchronize it with the light clock. Your wristwatch, for example, probably measures time by the vibration of a small crystal. We have seen that atomic clocks measure time by the behavior of an electron in a cesium atom. In both cases we could adjust D in our light clock to make it tick at the same rate. We could even, in principle, adjust the light clock so that it flashed once a day or even once a year, although in those cases we'd have to move the mirror outside of the solar system.

So with the understanding that the results we derive for our light clock will hold for any other clock, let's proceed to our first simple *gedanken* experiment. Let's begin with an observer on the ground with a light clock whose mirror is a distance D from the flashbulb. Let us call T_G the time on the ground clock as seen by an observer on the ground. Let us call the time it takes the light to get from the flashbulb to the mirror one 'tick' on the ground clock (defining things this way is just a matter of convenience). Then clearly

$$T_G = D \ / \ c$$

where c, as always, is the speed of light.

The time registered on a clock by an observer in the same frame of reference as the clock is called the 'proper' time. This is simply a term that specifies the frame of the observer, and has no implication of 'right' or 'correct'.

Now let us suppose that there is an observer on a train moving to the right with constant speed v, and that that observer has an identical light clock, with a distance D between the mirror and the flashbulb. Finally, let us arrange things so that as the moving clock passes the observer on the ground, both flashbulbs go off. (Note that these events will be seen as simultaneous in both frames of reference, since they occur at the same point.) What will happen?

The ground observer will find his clock to be operating normally, with the light moving from the flashbulb to the mirror in a time T_G. The train observer will find the clock on the train behaving in the same way—both observers find that the clocks in their frames of reference are registering the proper time in their frame. The interesting question, though, is to ask how the observer on the ground sees the clock on the train operating. The flashbulb on the train, as we said, will go off as that clock passes the ground observer. While the light is traveling upward toward the mirror on the train, however, the train itself will be moving toward the right, so that the mirror on the train will have moved to the right by the time the light hits it. As measured by the ground observer, then, the light in the clock on the train is traveling on a slanting line. The same thing will happen as the light moves back down toward the photocell. Thus, the observer on the ground observes the light in the clock on the train traveling in a sawtooth pattern, while the light in the clock on the ground travels straight up and down.

This is a crucial point, because as far as the observer on the ground is concerned, the light in the clock on the train has to travel a longer distance between 'ticks' than the light in the clock on the ground. If the principle of relativity is correct and Maxwell's equations are the same in all frames of reference, then light will be moving at the same speed (c) in both frames. This can only mean that an observer on the ground will measure the light taking longer to get from the flashbulb to the mirror on the train than the time it takes for light to make the same trip in the clock on the ground. In other words, to an observer on the ground *the moving clock will be ticking more slowly.*

Before proceeding with the question of time dilation, let's ask a question to make sure we understand where we are. Given that the observer on the ground observes the moving clock slowing down, what does the observer on the train see? Is the ground clock ticking faster or slower than the one on the train? If you answered 'slower', you've understood the argument. If you didn't, convince yourself that an observer on the train observes his or her clock registering the proper time and sees the light in the ground clock traveling in a sawtooth to the left.

The slowing down of the moving clock is such a violation of our intuition (not to mention the ideas of Newton and Galileo) that we should take some time to discuss it, because if we can really understand this so-called time dilation, we will be well on the road to understanding special relativity.

The first thing we can do is find a quantitative relationship between T_G and the time on the moving clock as seen by an observer on the ground, which we can call T_M. The distance the light on the moving clock travels as seen by an observer on the ground (the slope of the sawtooth) will just be the hypotenuse of a triangle whose sides are D and vT_M (the distance the train travels while the light moves from the flashbulb to the mirror). From the Pythagorean Theorem, this is just

Distance $= \sqrt{D^2 + \left(vT_M\right)^2}$

so that the time it takes light to travel along this leg of the sawtooth (one 'tick' of the moving clock as *measured* by an observer on the ground) is just

$$T_M = \frac{\sqrt{D^2 + \left(vT_M\right)^2}}{c}$$

Using some simple algebra and remembering the definition of T_G, we can get the result that

$$T_M = \frac{T_G}{\sqrt{1 - \left(\dfrac{v}{c}\right)^2}}$$

That's it. We have just derived one of the most important results of special relativity using nothing but some simple algebra and the Pythagorean Theorem. It is because of the simplicity of this derivation and others like it that I said that the old legend that only a dozen people understand relativity is simply wrong.

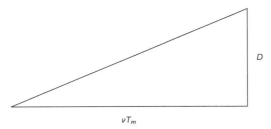

Figure 6.1 The path of light in the moving clock as seen by an observer on the ground

Looking at this result, we note that the expression inside the square root is always less than one. This means that T_M will always be bigger than T_G. More important, though, is that this equation represents a hard prediction. If it turns out that the two times are not related as in the equation, relativity will simply be wrong. As we shall see in Chapter 8, there is actually overwhelming evidence that the equation is correct, but at this stage of our discussion, the equation has to be regarded simply as a prediction to be tested against nature. In the slang used by physicists, the theoretical neck is on the chopping block.

It has been my experience that it is at this point in the development of relativity that many people want to get off the train. There seems to be something so wrong—so non-intuitive—about this result that our first reaction is often one of disbelief. This often takes the form of claiming that the moving clock hasn't 'really' slowed down. Let's examine this claim for a moment.

What people usually have in mind is that the clock on the train, *as measured by an observer on the train*, hasn't slowed down. This is absolutely true, but that's not what the equation is about. The equation deals with the time registered on the moving clock *as measured by an observer on the ground*. The use of the word 'really' implies that there is a clock in a preferred frame of reference that, like the blind fish in the Caspian Sea we mentioned at the beginning of Chapter 5, keeps the correct time. We can imagine universes in which that might be true, but the real question is whether the universe we actually live in behaves that way. As we have stressed repeatedly, that is a question that can only be answered by experiment and observation.

Another way of approaching the non-intuitive nature of time dilation is to think about where our intuition comes from. We live in a Newtonian world of normal-sized objects moving at normal speeds, and our intuition is based on our experiences with that world. None of us has ever traveled at an appreciable fraction of the speed of light, so none of us can claim to have an intuition about what it would be like to do so. Considering the equation we derived, however, we note that for speeds that are small compared with c (i.e. all speeds on which our intuition is based), T_M and T_G will be virtually identical. If the train was moving at 60 miles per hour, for example, it would take about ten million years for the time on the two clocks to differ by one second. You wouldn't expect, in other words, that you would observe time dilation when you're driving past a clock on a roadside building. Only very accurate clocks could detect such a small effect, and it should come as no surprise that time dilation is neither part of our experience nor of our intuition.

It's also important to realize that when the speed of the moving clock is small compared with the speed of light, so that the prediction of relativity is that $T_M = T_G$, we recover the Newtonian–Galilean result that moving clocks keep the same time as stationary ones. This fact actually illustrates an important point about relativity. It is often portrayed as a theoretical development that 'replaces' Newtonian physics. This is simply not the case. We should think instead about relativity as *extending* Newtonian physics.

Here's why. Every scientific law is only as good as the data that backs it up. The extensive data supporting classical physics are all gathered from the observation of normal-sized objects moving at normal speeds—speeds well below that of light. The standard laws of classical physics described in Chapter 2 describe this world to a very high level of accuracy. This is why we still teach Newtonian physics to students who will go on to build bridges, guide spacecraft, and become physicians. Newton's Laws still operate in the region for which data supports them.

If you ask whether these same laws operate near the speed of light, however, you run into a problem. In the nineteenth century, there was simply no data to answer this question, either in the affirmative or the negative. It could be that the laws apply everywhere, but it could also be that new laws apply in the new region. Moving into areas where there is no data is a little like getting on an airplane in the United States. You depart from an airport where people are speaking English. When you get off that plane, however, people may be speaking English or they may not be—it depends on where you land. In the same way, departing from the firm base of classical physics into the new region of high speeds may land you in a place where Newton's Laws still apply or it may not—you won't know until you get off the plane.

But one thing we do know is that if the laws are indeed different in this new area, when we extrapolate those new laws down to the region of very low speeds they had better reduce to the old laws of classical physics. This is why the above remark about the time dilation equation is so important. It shows explicitly that Newtonian ideas about the behavior of clocks do not apply when speeds approach c. Nevertheless, when speeds are small compared with c, the equations of relativity reduce to the Newtonian result.

This is, in fact, a general feature of the great revolutionary advances of twentieth-century physics. Just as relativity extends Newtonian physics to the realm of high speeds, quantum mechanics extends them to the realm of the very small. In both cases, however, if the new laws are applied to normal-sized objects moving at normal speeds, they reduce to the classical results.

I like to think that the growth of science is something like the growth of a tree. New material is added on the periphery, but the heartwood does not change. Think of relativity as the new growth and classical physics as the heartwood and you have a good picture of the relationship between Einstein and Newton.

With this general philosophical framework in mind, we can return to the program laid out in Chapter 5, where we argued that one way to approach the apparent contradiction between Newton and Maxwell was to re-examine our notions of space and time. The equation for time dilation outlined above shows that the notion of time does indeed change if we demand that the speed of light be the same in all frames of reference. What about our notions of space?

The fundamental aspect of space is the measurement of length, and we will use the words 'length' and 'space' more or less interchangeably in what follows. This time our *gedanken* experiment will involve two pieces of apparatus. One will be a clock—it can be a light clock, a stopwatch, or any other timepiece. The other will be our familiar flashbulb-mirror-photocell, laid out so that the light travels in a horizontal direction. In this experiment, in addition, the flashbulb fires only once. The light travels to the mirror and back, and we use the clock to determine how long it takes to do so.

An observer on the ground with this equipment is ready to measure length. Suppose the flashbulb and mirror are located at the two ends of a yardstick of length L_G. Then the time it takes for the light to go up and back will be

$$T_G = 2L_G / c$$

so that the length of the yardstick is just

$$L_G = cT_G / 2$$

In this analysis we have used the subscript 'G' to indicate that we are talking about a situation in which both the observer and the experiment are in a frame of reference on the ground. In analogy with the definition of proper time, L_G is called the 'proper length' of the yardstick.

Although the introduction of the light clock may have seemed like a strange way to measure time, the experiment we've just described is actually, in principle, the way length is defined these days, as we discussed in the last chapter. Consequently, we don't have to go through the same type of justification for our method of measuring length that we did for our measurement of time.

Now let's once again imagine two identical experiments, one on the ground and one on a train moving to the right with velocity v, and once again let's arrange things so that both flashbulbs go off when the flashbulb on the train passes the one on the ground. Once again, both the observer on the ground and the observer on the train will see their apparatus measuring the proper length, and once again the interesting question concerns what the observer on the ground sees happening in the apparatus on the train.

Here's the sequence as seen from the ground: the flashbulb on the train goes off and the light starts to move toward the mirror. While it is in transit, however, the mirror will be moving away from it with speed v—essentially, the light will be chasing the mirror. After the light is reflected, it will be moving to the left and the photocell will be approaching it with speed v. Thus the distance traveled by the light in the moving apparatus *as measured by an observer on the ground* will be different than the distance traveled by light in the apparatus on the ground.

The observer on the ground can then add up the travel time he or she measures in the moving system and use them to define the length of the moving yardstick—a length we'll call L_M. Remember that as far as the ground observer is concerned, the apparatus in his or her frame of reference is behaving normally and returning a length measurement of L_G. If that observer adds up the times on the train and takes into account the effects of time dilation, we find that the length of the moving yardstick as measured by an observer on the ground is given by

$$L_M = L_G \sqrt{1 - \left(\frac{v}{c}\right)^2}$$

In other words:

Moving objects are shortened in the direction of their motion.

A basketball moving near the speed of light, in other words, can be thought of as a pancake.

All the comments we made about time dilation can be applied to this so-called length contraction equation. The moving observer sees his or her own yardstick as having the proper length and the ground yardstick as contracted. When the speed v is small compared with the speed of light, L_M and L_G are essentially equal, so once again the equations of relativity reduce to the Newtonian result when they are applied to the Newtonian world.

The results of the above equation are often referred to as the 'Lorentz' contraction. As we saw in Chapter 4, the Dutch physicist Hendrik Lorentz proposed that an object moving through the ether would be shortened by this amount. For Lorentz, however, this was simply an *ad hoc* assumption needed to explain the lack of a result in the Michelson–Morley experiment, based on the idea that motion through the ether would cause the shortening. The alternative explanation—that there is no ether—is accepted today, but was unacceptable to Lorentz. As you can see from our derivations of time dilation and length contraction, however, Einstein's results rest on a firm theoretical foundation. If the principle of relativity is true and the speed of light is the same in all frames of reference, they follow from simple theoretical arguments.

We began our exploration of relativity with a simple conundrum—the question of what observers on a train and on the ground would measure for the speed of light emitted from a flashlight on the train. We argued that one possible resolution would be to retain the principle of relativity and Maxwell's equation and to re-examine our notions of space and time. Speed, after all, is just distance (length) divided by time, and we have seen that both of these quantities are different for the two observers. With this in mind we can now re-visit that conundrum.

Suppose a train-spotter standing beside a track observes a train moving with constant velocity, traveling to the right with fixed speed v. Now suppose an observer on the train throws a ball to the right with speed u_T as measured on the train. What will the speed—call it u_G—of that ball be as measured by the trackside train-spotter?

Arguments not that different from those used to derive time dilation and length contraction lead to the result

$$u_G = (u_T + v) \ / \ (1 + u_T v / c^2)$$

Again, we note that if the speeds are small compared with the speed of light, we simply add the speed of the ball and the speed of the train, as both our intuition and Newton tell us to do. If, however, we want to talk about the flashlight problem, then $u_T = c$ and the above equation reduces to

$$u_G = (c + v) / (1 + v / c) = c$$

In other words, both observers find the light moving with speed c, and hence both observers find the same Maxwell equations in their frame of reference, as demanded by the principle of relativity. This is how Einstein resolved the apparent contradiction between Newton and Maxwell. The solution is both profound and elegant, but at the risk of being repetitive, it has to be verified by experiment before it can be accepted, a point to which we will return in Chapter 8.

We can close this chapter by noting, with Einstein, that the principle of relativity can play a powerful heuristic role in science. It is often the case that general principles can be used to winnow out concepts, ideas, and theories in the sciences. For example, you may remember from high school chemistry that the number of atoms of a specific type in a chemical reaction has to remain the same—if you start with three oxygen atoms, you have to finish with three oxygen atoms. This is a general principle that allows us to choose between theories of chemical reactions. If we had a theory that allowed the number of atoms of a specific type to change during a chemical reaction, we would be justified in throwing it out on general grounds, and not even subject it to experimental test. The test would, after all, just be a waste of time.

In the same way, Einstein argues, theories that do not incorporate the principle of relativity can be discarded *ab initio*. No matter how cleverly they are constructed, they simply cannot describe the universe we live in. Indeed, all of the theories that are in competition for what is called the 'Theory of Everything', the final theory of the universe, have the principle built into them from the very start.

With this, we can now turn our attention to more results from special relativity, results which at least in one case, are considerably more famous that those we've derived so far.

7

MORE RESULTS FROM SPECIAL RELATIVITY

EINSTEIN'S *RELATIVITY* CHAPTERS 15 AND 17

$E = mc^2$
   Albert Einstein

In the first of these chapters, Einstein presents the most famous result of the theory of relativity, the mass–energy equation. In the second of the chapters he gives a short discussion of the so-called Minkowski diagrams, which give us a simple visual way to analyze relativistic events.

It's interesting that Einstein's original paper on special relativity was 31 pages long, but the 1905 paper that introduced the above equation contained only three pages, despite the fact that this equation has, in effect, left the realm of physics and become something of a cultural icon. It is, in fact, the only physics equation you might reasonably expect the man on the street to recognize, if not understand. Let's look at the background to this equation before we go into Einstein's derivation of it.

As we saw in Chapter 2, in the mid-nineteenth century the science of thermodynamics was put into its final form. We also saw that there were three important facts about energy:

- It comes in many forms.
- The forms are interchangeable.
- The energy of a closed system cannot change.

The consequences of these facts are all around us. Energy in the form of sunlight fell to Earth millions of years ago and was converted to stored chemical energy by the process of photosynthesis in plants. Over the millennia geological forces converted the remains of those plants to coal, and a few months ago that coal was mined and taken to an electrical generating plant. There it was burned and the stored chemical energy was converted to heat which was used to produce steam. The steam was used to turn a turbine as the thermal energy was converted to rotational energy, and the rotational energy was converted to the energy in an electric current. This current was sent out over wires to your house, and when you flipped a light switch the electrical energy was converted to light and heat. Eventually the energy from the light bulb will be converted into infrared radiation and sent back out into space to continue its interrupted journey. According to the laws of thermodynamics, then, you are just one actor in an infinite chain of events involving the conversion of energy from one form to another—a chain in which energy is neither created nor destroyed. In this picture, you can think of the energy of any system as being a reservoir of ever-changing forms, but a reservoir whose total volume never changes.

At the same time, scientists were realizing that there was another great reservoir in nature. We alluded to this at the end of the last chapter, when we talked about balancing chemical equations and pointed out that the number of atoms of a given species that are present at the start of a chemical reaction has to be the same as the number present at the end. This is, in fact, an example of what is called the conservation of mass. This principle states that the quantity of mass in a closed system cannot change over time. Like energy, you can think of mass as constituting another vast reservoir.

So at the start of the twentieth century, scientists saw the world as containing two reservoirs, energy and mass, but thought of each of them as self-contained and isolated. What Einstein's revolutionary equation showed was that there is, in fact, a bridge between these two reservoirs— that energy can be converted into mass and mass can be converted into energy. When he wrote his book in the early 1930s, there was no evidence to back up this idea—it was simply another prediction that would have to be verified. Today, we see this bridge operating in both directions every day. In nuclear reactors around the world a fraction of the mass of uranium atoms is converted into energy by the process of nuclear fission, ultimately producing electricity—20 percent of the electricity consumed in the United States is produced in this way, for example. At the same time at accelerator laboratories, particles like protons are accelerated to almost the speed of light and their kinetic energy is converted into a mass of elementary particles. Thus, the experimental verification of this famous equation is an established fact of nature.

Many scholars prefer to think of the equation in a slightly different way, and to argue that it establishes mass as just another form of energy which can be interchanged with other forms. From this point of view, there is just one reservoir—energy—and mass takes its place with the other forms in it.

Unfortunately, the mass–energy equation cannot be derived from simple geometrical considerations like those we used to derive time dilation and length contraction. We can, however, get some sense of where it comes from by thinking about a quintessentially Newtonian problem, the collision of two billiard balls. As always, we will observe the collision from two frames of reference—one on the ground and the other moving with speed u.

At this point we have to make an important distinction. Although in everyday speech the terms 'speed' and 'velocity' are used interchangeably, in physics they have slightly different meanings. 'Speed' refers to *how fast something is moving*, e.g. '10 miles per hour'. Velocity refers to *how fast something is moving and the direction of that motion*, e.g. '10 miles per hour due north'.

In Newtonian physics, a particle of mass m moving with speed v will have kinetic energy $\frac{1}{2}mv^2$ and momentum of magnitude mv in its direction of motion. The total momentum of a system is the sum of the momenta of the individual particles, taking directions into account, and it follows from Newton's Laws that the total momentum of the system is the same before and after the collision (although the momenta of individual billiard balls can change). The same will be true of kinetic energy if there are no additional sources of sinks of energy in the system. (Physicists call such a collision 'elastic'.)

If an observer on the ground sees a billiard ball moving with speed v, then an observer in the moving frame will see it moving with speed $v + u$. Some simple algebra shows that in this case both momentum and kinetic energy will be conserved in the moving frame. In the jargon of physics, we say that these laws are 'covariant'.

As we saw in the last chapter, however, the rules for the addition of velocities in relativity are more complicated that the simple addition that characterizes the Newtonian world. In the relativistic world, the Newtonian expressions for momentum and kinetic energy will not be covariant. This means that we have to find new expressions for these quantities, and whatever those expressions are, they had better (1) be covariant, and (2) reduce to the Newtonian expressions for small velocities.

What Einstein did in his paper was to find just such expressions. His result was a redefinition of momentum magnitude and energy in the following forms:

$$\text{Momentum} = \frac{m_0 v}{\sqrt{1 - \left(\dfrac{v}{c}\right)^2}}$$

and

$$\text{Energy} = mc^2$$

where

$$m = \frac{m_0}{\sqrt{1 - \left(\dfrac{v}{c}\right)^2}}$$

and m_0 is the mass of the particle as measured by an observer in the same frame. This quantity is referred to as the 'rest mass' of the particle.

At this point we run into a historical problem. In the traditional interpretation of Einstein's results, we talk about the mass of a particle increasing with velocity, as above. In modern presentations, however, it has become customary to keep the discussion in terms of energy and momentum. In what follows I will stay with the traditional interpretation, both because this is what Einstein used and because I have found, from a pedagogical point of view, that the modern interpretation introduces a level of abstraction that many students find difficult. The translation of arguments involving mass to arguments involving momentum and energy is pretty straightforward, and I leave it as an exercise for the reader.

There are many consequences of the above equations, and we will address them one at a time.

AVAILABLE ENERGY

In the first place, c is a large number, so that the conversion of small amounts of mass will produce large amounts of energy. The fact that a grapefruit-sized piece of enriched uranium (of which a chunk the size of a dime is converted into energy) has enough explosive power to destroy a city is an indication of this fact. On a more peaceful note, the mass of a single grain of sand, if it were converted completely to energy, would be enough to supply the energy needs of several houses for a year, and the energy in a pile of sand that would fit under your desk could power a large city for the same amount of time. The ultimate expression of Einstein's equation, albeit a fictional one, can be seen in the *Starship Enterprise* in the *Star Trek* series. The ship is powered by matter and matter annihilating, a process that converts all of the mass of the matter and antimatter particles into energy.

As Einstein points out, for small values of v the expression for energy can be approximated by

$E = m_0 c^2 + \frac{1}{2} mv^2 +$ higher order terms in v/c

This expression can be understood in a simple way. The first term, referred to as the 'rest energy' of the object, represents the energy locked up in its mass. The second term, of course, represents the standard energy of motion—kinetic energy. If v/c is much less than one, as it is for most familiar objects, the rest of the terms in the expansion can be ignored.

Finally, we note that although the mass–energy equation is most often thought of in terms of nuclear and particle interactions, in fact it applies to all forms of energy. A cocked mousetrap, for example, has an (infinitesimally) higher mass than a mousetrap that is not cocked. The association of the equation with nuclear and particle processes arises because it is only in those processes that the conversion of mass to energy (and vice versa) occurs at an appreciable level.

THE UNIVERSAL SPEED LIMIT

One bit of folklore that is familiar to every science fiction buff is the statement that nothing can move faster than the speed of light. At this point in our discussion we can explore the basis for this statement.

Look at the above expression for mass. Because the expression in the square root is always less than one, for a moving body m will always be bigger than m_0. We can say, in analogy to our statements about time dilation and length contraction

The mass of a moving body increases with speed.

In fact, if you look at the equation, you will realize that the faster an object moves, the more massive it becomes. This, in turn, means that as the speed of an object increases, the force needed to accelerate it further increases as well. In fact, you can see that to get an object up to the speed of light would require an infinite force. Consequently we can say that

No object now moving at less than c can be accelerated to light speed.

Having stated the universal speed limit in this way, we note that there are important statements that can be made:

- It does not imply that nothing can move at the speed of light.
- It does not imply that nothing can move faster than the speed of light.

The first statement is obvious, because we already know of something that travels at the speed of light—light itself. The reason for this is that the rest mass of the photon is zero, so that the expression for the mass of the photons takes the mathematical form of $0/0$, which need not be infinite. (To see this, consider the limit of x/x as x approaches zero. The ratio remains one even though we seem to be dividing by zero.)

For a long time physicists thought that another particle, known as the neutrino, also had zero mass and traveled at speed c. It has turned out, however, that neutrinos have a small mass and travel at speeds slightly less than c.

The second point is also simple. If there is an object now moving faster than the speed of light, an argument similar to that given above shows that it can never be decelerated to a speed less than the speed of light. Over the years physicists have speculated about the possibility that such particles might exist, and a few attempts to detect them have been made, without success. Such particles are called 'tachyons' (from the same Greek root that gives us 'tachometer'). In this scheme, objects like ourselves that always move at less than the speed of light are called 'tardyons' or 'bradyons' (from the Greek root for 'slow'). The idea of tachyons arises because, in the language of some theorists, the speed of light is indeed the limit, but every limit has two sides, so that the world of tachyons would be sort of a mirror image of our own. Science fiction aside, however, there is no evidence whatsoever that tachyons exist.

So where do phenomena like the fictional warp drive fit in? The easiest way to picture how it might work is to imagine a piece of paper with two points on it—call them A and B. If we were two-dimensional beings, we could only get from A to B by moving across the paper, where we presumably couldn't travel faster than the speed of light. If we folded the paper over, however, so that A was on top of B, and if we left our two-dimensional world for a moment, we could step into the third dimension and move from A to B instantaneously. To a two-dimensional being confined to the paper this would look miraculous—we would disappear from A and appear at B without ever traversing the paper between them. This kind of fictional travel was well described by the author Isaac Asimov in his book *Foundation*:

> Through hyperspace, that unimaginable region that was neither space nor time, matter nor energy, something nor nothing, one could traverse the galaxy between two neighboring instants of time.

Recently, speculation about a faster-than-light drive has picked up, with physicists suggesting systems where ships are enclosed in a space-time bubble. In this scheme the ship moves at normal speeds inside the bubble, but the bubble moves at superluminal speeds, something like someone walking on one of those moving sidewalks at an airport.

Is it likely that there will anything like this in our future? Who knows? All we can say is that right now there is no basis in science for the existence of anything like hyperspace or warp drives.

EINSTEIN AND THE ATOMIC BOMB

As we pointed out in Chapter 1, Einstein was a lifelong pacifist. His position modified somewhat in the 1930s, after Hitler came into power in Germany, though, and that's where his famous letter to President Roosevelt came in.

When mass–energy equivalence was first proposed, no one thought about nuclear fission as a possible outcome of the result—after all, the discovery of the nucleus was still years in the future. In 1938, however, the German physicists Otto Hahn and Fritz Strassman published the results of an experiment in which they had bombarded uranium nuclei with neutrons and found the element barium in the debris of the collision. (Hahn was later awarded the Nobel Prize for this work.) This could only mean that they had split the uranium nucleus through a process that came to be called 'fission'. It became immediately apparent to many physicists, particularly to Leo Szilard, an old colleague of Einstein's who had fled his native Hungary to escape the Nazis, that the fission process could produce massive amounts of energy. Szilard, in fact, had been speculating about the possibility of using fission to create a chain reaction in uranium. This, of course, is the basis of what would become the atomic bomb.

When the Germans halted the export of uranium from mines in Czechoslovakia, Szilard, eventually joined by fellow Hungarian émigrés Eugene Wigner and Edward Teller, began to worry about how to warn the world about the possibility that the Nazis might develop a weapon based on nuclear fission. At first they considered approaching the Belgian ambassador in Washington about exports of uranium from what was then the Belgian Congo, but they were soon persuaded to approach President Roosevelt instead.

This is where Einstein's fame and international status came in. As we pointed out in Chapter 1, he had become a household name in America, and anything he said would be taken very seriously indeed. He was the obvious person to send the warning to Roosevelt. After some discussion, Einstein dictated a letter to Roosevelt (in German—it was translated by Szilard) dated August 2, 1939—see Figure 7.1. The key part of the letter read:

> ... it may become possible to set up a nuclear chain reaction in a large mass of uranium, by which vast amounts of power...would be generated. Now it appears almost certain that this could be achieved in the immediate future.
>
> This new phenomenon would also lead to the construction of bombs and it is conceivable—though much less certain—that extremely powerful bombs of a new type might thus be constructed.

Albert Einstein
Old Grove Rd.
Nassau Point
Peconic, Long Island

August 2nd, 1939

F.D. Roosevelt,
President of the United States,
White House
Washington, D.C.

Sir:

Some recent work by E.Fermi and L. Szilard, which has been com-
municated to me in manuscript, leads me to expect that the element uranium may be turned into a new and important source of energy in the immediate future. Certain aspects of the situation which has arisen seem
to call for watchfulness and, if necessary, quick action on the part
of the Administration. I believe therefore that it is my duty to bring
to your attention the following facts and recommendations:

In the course of the last four months it has been made probable -
through the work of Joliot in France as well as Fermi and Szilard in
America - that it may become possible to set up a nuclear chain reaction
in a large mass of uranium,by which vast amounts of power and large quantities of new radium-like elements would be generated. Now it appears
almost certain that this could be achieved in the immediate future.

This new phenomenon would also lead to the construction of bombs,
and it is conceivable - though much less certain - that extremely powerful bombs of a new type may thus be constructed. A single bomb of this
type, carried by boat and exploded in a port, might very well destroy
the whole port together with some of the surrounding territory. However,
such bombs might very well prove to be too heavy for transportation by
air.

Figure 7.1 Einstein's letter to Roosevelt dated August 2, 1939

-2-

The United States has only very poor ores of uranium in moderate quantities. There is some good ore in Canada and the former Czechoslovakia, while the most important source of uranium is Belgian Congo.

In view of this situation you may think it desirable to have some permanent contact maintained between the Administration and the group of physicists working on chain reactions in America. One possible way of achieving this might be for you to entrust with this task a person who has your confidence and who could perhaps serve in an inofficial capacity. His task might comprise the following:

a) to approach Government Departments, keep them informed of the further development, and put forward recommendations for Government action, giving particular attention to the problem of securing a supply of uranium ore for the United States;

b) to speed up the experimental work,which is at present being carried on within the limits of the budgets of University laboratories, by providing funds, if such funds be required, through his contacts with private persons who are willing to make contributions for this cause, and perhaps also by obtaining the co-operation of industrial laboratories which have the necessary equipment.

I understand that Germany has actually stopped the sale of uranium from the Czechoslovakian mines which she has taken over. That she should have taken such early action might perhaps be understood on the ground that the son of the German Under-Secretary of State, von Weizsäcker, is attached to the Kaiser-Wilhelm-Institut in Berlin where some of the American work on uranium is now being repeated.

Yours very truly,

(Albert Einstein)

Roosevelt sent a reply and set up a commission to look into the issues Einstein raised. Not much happened at first—in fact Einstein sent him three more letters urging action. What seems to have finally triggered the activity that led to the Manhattan Project and the atomic bomb was a 1940 report from the so-called MAUD committee in Britain (the acronym stands for 'Military Applications of Uranium Detonation'), which estimated that a fission bomb would need only a few pounds of uranium to operate. It was at this point that the Manhattan Project came into existence.

Contrary to popular folklore, then, Einstein did not singlehandedly start the program that led to the atomic bomb. Instead, his letter to Roosevelt prepared the ground for the rapid acceptance of the MAUD report. Ironically, Einstein himself played a very small role in the Manhattan Project, carrying out only a few minor calculations on uranium isotope separation. Some authors have suggested that his well-known pacifist views created the fear that he would be a security risk. My own sense is that this is unlikely, given the level of espionage that was eventually uncovered at Los Alamos—security just wasn't that tight. It's more likely, I think, that Einstein simply realized that his type of expertise was not what was needed in the project.

MINKOWSKI DIAGRAMS

Hermann Minkowski (1864–1909) was born in a rural village in an area that had once been part of the Polish–Lithuanian Commonwealth but had passed under the control of Russia after the partitions of Poland that took place between 1772 and 1795. As befits his birth in a region of questionable political ties, various biographers have described his ethnicity as either Lithuanian, Polish, German, or Russian. In any case, he was educated in the German university system and he eventually became a lecturer in mathematics at the ETH in Zurich (see Chapter 1), where the young Albert Einstein was one of his students.

Minkowski's main research interests revolved around finding geometrical interpretations of mathematical problems. In 1907, two years after Einstein published his paper on special relativity, Minkowski realized that there was a simple geometrical way to think about relativistic events. It's easiest to explain this in two dimensions, but a full-blown treatment would demand four dimensions—three of space and one of time.

To construct a two-dimensional Minkowski space, imagine a Cartesian coordinate system in which the horizontal axis represents the position on an object in space, and the vertical axis represents the position in time. Let the origin (0, 0) define the location of the object right now. We'll label this point 'The Present'.

If the object doesn't move, time will still go by. This means that the point representing the object will move straight up on the vertical axis. If the object moves in space as well, the point that represents it will move to the left or right as it moves upward in time. If the velocity is constant, the point will trace out a sloping line on the graph. A particularly important pair of lines are the ones corresponding to an object moving at the speed of light. These two lines (one leaning toward the right, the other toward the left) enclose the points on the graph that an object traveling at less than the speed of light can reach (to reach outside of the lines the object would have to move faster than light). The volume of space inside this so-called 'light cone', then, represents a region we can call 'The Future'. The region outside the light cone represents areas that cannot be reached from 'The Present' and is usually labeled 'Elsewhere'.

This same sort of analysis can be extended backwards in time as well. The region inside the downward sloping light cone represents all points in the past that could reach 'The Present'. This region can be called 'The Past', while the region outside the light cone is also 'Elsewhere'.

The Minkowski diagram thus provides a simple way of visualizing relativistic events and processes, and is often used as a supplement to more abstract mathematical discussions. Its primary importance is that it represents a simple way of seeing that time must be treated as a coordinate on an equal footing with space. In Minkowski's words (from the 80th Assembly of German Natural Scientists and Physicians, 21 September 1908):

> The views of space and time which I wish to lay before you have sprung from the soil of experimental physics, and therein lies their strength. They are radical. Henceforth space by itself, and time by itself, are doomed to fade away into mere shadows, and only a kind of union of the two will preserve an independent reality.

Finally, we note that the Minkowski diagram also gives an intuitive meaning to the term 'spacetime', which implies that time is on an equal footing with the traditional three spatial dimensions.

8

EXPERIMENTAL PROOFS OF SPECIAL RELATIVITY
EINSTEIN'S *RELATIVITY* CHAPTER 16

Merely corroborative details to lend an aspect of verisimilitude to what
would otherwise be a bald and unconvincing narrative.

W.S. Gilbert and Arthur Sullivan, *The Mikado*

Einstein spends comparatively little time discussing the experimental
tests of special relativity, concentrating on length contraction and the
Michelson–Morley experiment. A great deal of evidence has been gathered
since he wrote his book.

Having gone through our mathematical exploration of the consequences
of the postulates of special relativity, we now have some serious predictions
that can be tested. In a sense, this is the point where we had to arrive, the
point at which we match our ideas against nature, the ultimate arbiter. For
the sake of completeness, we list the key predictions of relativity below:

- Moving clocks slow down.
- Moving objects contract in the direction of motion.
- The mass of moving objects increases with speed.
- $E = mc^2$.

In the previous chapter we reviewed the overwhelming evidence supporting the last item in the list—the equivalence of mass and energy—so we will not return to that subject here. Einstein himself spends relatively little time on the question of experimental verification of relativity. Partly this is because most of the experiments we will discuss were done after his book was written. I can't help but think, though, that his orientation as a theoretical physicist had something to do with this apparent neglect as well. He is, after all, supposed to have replied to the question of what he would do if the experiments didn't verify his theory with the remark, 'Then I would feel sorry for God.'

There are two types of experiments we will discuss. One set involves the unsuccessful search for the ether, since the absence of a 'God's eye' frame of reference is a necessary prerequisite to relativity. The other set involves direct tests of the other predictions. In addition, in some cases we will have to distinguish between the predictions of special and general relativity. The latter will be dealt with in more detail in Chapter 12.

THE SEARCH FOR THE ETHER

In retrospect, the most important ether search was the Michelson–Morley experiment, which we discussed in some detail in Chapter 4. The lack of a positive result in this experiment was a thorn in the side of physicists for decades, as Kelvin's 'dark cloud' speech shows. As we saw, the result could be explained by assuming that objects moving through the ether were shortened in their direction of motion—an effect that was later explained in terms of relativistic length contraction. In 1932, a follow-on experiment was carried out by the American physicists Roy Kennedy and Edward Thorndike, who were at the University of Washington and Polytechnic Institute of Brooklyn, respectively. It differed from the Michelson–Morley experiment in only one detail—the distances traveled by the two light beams were different, rather than being the same. For technical reasons, it requires both length contraction and time dilation for an apparatus of this type to yield a null result. The fact that Kennedy and Thorndike found no evidence for ether wind as the Earth moved in its orbit and revolved around its axis was taken as further evidence for the absence of a preferred frame of reference. Since then, experiments of this type have been carried out with various modern techniques, such as lasers and masers, and they all yield the same result.

An earlier experiment that Einstein said did influence his thinking was carried out by the French physicist Hippolyte Fizeau (1819–1896) in 1851. His goal was to measure the speed of light in moving water, a quantity that in the mid-nineteenth century would be expected to be the sum of the speed of light in stationary water and the speed of the water.

Before we get into the details of Fizeau's experiment, we should take a moment to discuss the propagation of light through material objects. The quantity we have called 'c' is the speed of light in a vacuum. When light moves through a material, however, it is constantly being absorbed and re-emitted by atoms in the material, so its speed will be less than c. A good analogy is to compare the time it takes a non-stop flight to cross a continent to the time it takes if the passenger has to change planes at a couple of airports. The second passenger will arrive at the destination later than the first, so that we would say that he or she traveled more slowly, even though the speed of all the airplanes was the same while they were actually in motion. In the same way, the net effect of the absorption and re-emission of light by atoms in a material results in a slower overall progress of the light. We generally express this by saying that u, the speed of light in matter, is given by $u = c/n$, where 'n' is a quantity known as the index of refraction. For reference, the index of refraction of glass is around 1.5, which means that light travels roughly 50 percent slower in glass than in a vacuum.

In Fizeau's apparatus, a beam of light was split in two. The beams then entered a tube in which water was circulating. For the sake of definiteness, let's say that the beams are moving to the left, and the circulation of the water is such that water in the upper part of the tube is moving to the left and the water in the lower part of the tube is moving toward the right. Let's suppose that the upper part of the split light beam goes through the top of the tube. After exiting, a system of lenses and mirrors then sends it back through the bottom part of the tube. This part of the beam, then, will always be traveling in the same direction as the water. In a similar way, the other half of the beam will always be moving in the opposite direction from the water.

This means that the Newtonian prediction if the water were moving at speed v would be that the upper beam should be traveling at a velocity $v + c/n$ and the lower beam should be traveling at a speed $v - c/n$. The two beams, which started out synchronized, should therefore arrive back at the starting point at different times, an effect that is easy to measure with standard optical techniques.

When Fizeau, a careful and respected experimenter, got his results he was truly puzzled. He found that the movement of the water had some effect on the light, but not the effect he expected. For light traveling with the water, for example, the speed according to Newton should be $v + c/n$— the speed of light in water plus the speed of the water. What Fizeau found was that the speed was $c/n + v\,(1 - 1/n^2)$, while for light traveling against the water it was $c/n - v\,(1 - 1/n^2)$.

The measured effect was actually much smaller than expected. It was, in fact, in line with a suggestion that had been made earlier by the French physicist and mathematician Augustine-Jean Fresnel (1788–1827). Fresnel had argued that the movement of the water through the ether dragged the ether along, but only partially. While Fizeau's result seemed to verify this prediction, the whole explanation was so contrived that it was almost universally rejected by physicists. Here are Fizeau's (1851) own words on the subject:

> The success of the experiment seems to me to render the adoption of Fresnel's hypothesis necessary, or at least the law which he found for the expression of the alteration of the velocity of light by the effect of motion of a body; for although that law being found true may be a very strong proof in favor of the hypothesis of which it is only a consequence, perhaps the conception of Fresnel may appear so extraordinary, and in some respects so difficult, to admit, that other proofs and a profound examination on the part of geometricians will still be necessary before adopting it as an expression of the real facts of the case.
>
> 'Sur les hypothèses relatives à l'éther lumineux.'
> *Comptes Rendus* 33: 349–355

There were many reasons to be distrustful of the ether drag hypothesis. For one thing, the drag would have to be slightly different for different wavelengths of light. For another, in 1893 the British physicist Oliver Lodge (1851–1948) did experiments where he spun a heavy iron disk under an optical experiment and found that the disk produced no change in the optics, as it would if ether were being dragged.

Shortly after Einstein published his paper on relativity, however, people realized that Fizeau's result was a simple consequence of the formula for the addition of velocities that we wrote down in an earlier chapter. If we let $u = c/n$ be the speed of light in stationary water (what we called u_T in Chapter 6) and v be the speed of water, then the equation for the addition of velocities tells us that u_G, the speed of light as measured by an observer on the ground, will just be

$$u_G = (v + c/n)/\left(1 + (c/n)(v/c)\right)$$

which, for small v/c, is approximately equal to $c/n + v\,(1 - 1/n^2)$ which is Fizeau's result. (Note that Einstein does this same calculation in his Chapter 13.)

Thus we have another case where relativity clears up a puzzling mystery in classical physics. The 'other proofs and a profound examination' that Fizeau wanted turned out to be nothing more than special relativity!

TIME DILATION

Other than the effects of mass–energy equivalence, the most dramatic verifications of special relativity are those involving time dilation. These proofs seem to have a profound effect on people because they speak to what is most often regarded as the most counter-intuitive of Einstein's predictions. In what follows, we will deal with the most dramatic of these experiments first, then move on to some that are perhaps more fundamental. I should also note in passing that because of space limitations I will be discussing only a fraction of the experiments that have actually been carried out.

AIRPLANE EXPERIMENTS

By far the most direct test of time dilation was carried out in October 1971 by Joseph Hafele, a physicist then at Washington University in Saint Louis, and Richard Keating, an astronomer at the U.S. Naval Observatory in Washington DC. The basic logic of their experiment was to put atomic clocks on airplanes that were flying around the world and compare the elapsed time those clocks measured against the time measured on atomic clocks left behind at the U.S. Naval Observatory.

According to physics legend, the scientists convinced Pan American Airlines (which is no longer in existence) to give them seats on Pan Am 1 (which went around the world by traveling east) and Pan Am 2 (which went around the world traveling west). There is, in fact, a wonderful photograph of a smiling flight attendant next to two atomic clocks and a physicist on one of the planes. The result of the experiment was striking— after their trips, the atomic clocks did indeed register a different time than the clock that had been stationary.

Several points need to be made about this result. In the first place, the differences in time were very small—hundreds of nanoseconds. This is indeed a small difference, but one well within the capability of atomic clocks to measure. (Remember that a nanosecond in 10^{-9} seconds and atomic clocks can be accurate to 10^{-13} seconds.) The second point is that both special and general relativity contribute to the time difference. The effect of time dilation from special relativity will result in the moving clock ticking more slowly. We will see in Chapter 13, however, that general relativity predicts an additional effect due to the fact that the gravitational potential at 30,000 feet, where the plane is flying, is different from the gravitational field on the ground. This effect works in the opposite direction from time dilation, and will make the clock in the airplane tick faster than the clock on the ground. (Remember, though, that the person in the airplane sees his or her clock ticking normally.) When all of these effects were taken into account, the differences between the flying clocks and their sedentary brothers were exactly as predicted by the theory.

While this quantitative agreement is a good outcome, my own sense is that the Hafele–Keating experiment has an importance that goes beyond numbers. The fact that moving clocks really do register a different time is a direct and dramatic demonstration of the fact that the Newtonian notion of a universal time is simply wrong, as is our intuition about the behavior of clocks.

This experiment has been repeated many times, with the same result. In 1975–76, scientists at the University of Maryland put atomic clocks into airplanes that made five flights of 15 hours each, and relativity came through with flying colors. In 1996, to mark the 25th anniversary of the original experiment, the Naval Observatory put up-to-date atomic clocks on flights from Washington to London and back to re-confirm the original results to a higher level of accuracy, and in 2010 the experiment was re-created in an around-the-world flight for British television.

PARTICLE EXPERIMENTS

A second confirmation of time dilation comes from the behavior of elementary particles. To understand these tests, we have to take a moment to talk about what was known about those particles in the mid-twentieth century.

In 1911, Ernest Rutherford, working at what is now the University of Manchester, showed that the atom had a nucleus. The nucleus of hydrogen, the lightest element, is a single positively charged particle called a proton ('first one'). From the fact that heavier nuclei had about twice as much mass as could be found in their protons, it was suggested that there was another particle in the nucleus—a particle that had about the same mass as the proton but no electrical charge. This particle was called the neutron ('neutral one') and was seen in experiments in 1932.

By the 1930s, then, physicists had a simple picture of the basic structure of the universe. The nucleus of the atom was made up of protons and neutrons, and the electrons in their orbits completed the atomic structure. Unfortunately, that simplicity was not destined to last.

The Earth is constantly being bombarded by particles from space—they're called cosmic rays. They are mostly protons and sometimes have very high energies indeed. When they hit atoms in the atmosphere, some of that energy is converted into the mass of other particles. Scientists began studying the debris of these collisions by putting instruments in labs located on mountaintops. In 1936, Carl Anderson and Seth Neidermeyer at the California Institute of Technology discovered something completely unexpected when a new kind of particle showed up in their apparatus.

This new particle was heavier than the electron but lighter than the proton and seemed to come in both positively and negatively charged varieties. Following theoretical work by the Japanese physicist Hideki Yukawa (1907–1981), whose ideas will be discussed in more detail in Chapter 10, the new particle was initially called a 'meson' ('middle one') because of its intermediate mass and denoted by the Greek letter 'mu' (μ). It turned out to be the first in a veritable zoo of elementary particles that would be discovered over the next fifty years, and is now known as the 'muon' (*mew*-on).

Like all of these new particles, the muon is unstable. A muon sitting on a table in front of you would disintegrate in a matter of microseconds, converting itself into an electron and a neutrino. And this is what gives us a chance to test time dilation, because the decay of the muon can be thought of as constituting a kind of clock—a clock that only ticks once, of course, but a clock nonetheless.

We can begin our analysis by asking how far a muon could travel after it is created if there were no time dilation. The fastest the particle could travel is 'c', or 3×10^8 meters/sec, so that in one microsecond (10^{-6} seconds) it could travel 300 meters (about 1000 feet). The test of time dilation is then obvious, because if we can demonstrate that muons travel farther than this before decaying, it can only be because the clock moving with the particle is ticking more slowly than the clock on the ground.

The first experiment of this type was done in 1940 by Bruno Rossi and David Hall of the University of Chicago. They measured the muon flux at Echo Lake in the Colorado Rockies and again in Denver, several thousand feet deeper into the atmosphere. The persistence of muons to the lower altitude was exactly as predicted by the special theory of relativity. The experiment was repeated at a higher level of accuracy in 1963, when David Frisch and James Smith of the Massachusetts Institute of Technology compared the muon flux on top of Mount Washington with the flux at sea level in Cambridge. Again, the results were exactly as predicted by special relativity. This particular experiment has become a fixture in undergraduate physics laboratories since then.

The persistence of muons and other unstable elementary particles at particle accelerator laboratories around the world has produced a mass of evidence for the reality of time dilation, with the accuracy of some experiments approaching eight decimal places. It is as well verified as any scientific effect can be.

GLOBAL POSITIONING SYSTEM

The final piece of evidence for time dilation that I want to discuss does not come from forefront physics experiments, but from engineering. Over the past couple of decades the Global Positioning System (GPS) has gone from being an experimental military system to something that is involved in everyday life. When you are on an airplane, for example, the pilot is keeping track of his or her position using GPS technology, and many modern cars use the system to give the driver directions on how to proceed through an onboard navigation system.

At heart, the GPS is a network of 24 satellites in orbits 20,000 km (12,000 miles) above the Earth, each moving at about 14,000 km/hr (8400 mph). On each of these satellites is an atomic clock calibrated to be accurate to about a nanosecond (10^{-9} seconds). In order to find its position on the Earth, a GPS receiver reads the time from several satellites (the orbits are such that at least four are always above the horizon) and combines this with knowledge of each satellite's position. If you think of the data from a single satellite as defining the surface of a sphere whose radius is the distance light could have traveled between the (known) time it left the satellite and the time it arrived at the receiver, then the position of the receiver is determined to be the intersection point of spheres from several satellites. Even a cheap hand-held receiver can locate its position to within 10 to 20 feet, and more sophisticated receivers can do better. This level of accuracy requires that the time on the clocks in the satellites must be known to a level of accuracy of around 20 nanoseconds.

There are two relativistic effects that affect the accuracy of the GPS system. Special relativity tells us that because of the motion of the satellites, the moving clocks will tick more slowly than clocks on the ground. Putting numbers into the time dilation equation tells us that the moving clocks will lose about 7 microseconds a day compared with clocks on the ground. As with the airplane experiments discussed above, the fact that the satellites are in a weaker gravitational field means that general relativity predicts that the moving clocks will run faster than those on the ground by about 45 microseconds per day.

Thus the net effect of relativity will be that the moving clocks will gain 45 − 7 = 38 microseconds per day. This effect, though small, is still 1000 times greater than the accuracy needed to determine positions as outlined above. If this were uncorrected, the errors in the GPS location would accumulate at the rate of roughly 10 km (6.7 miles) per day, so that after a month you might be standing in New York looking at a GPS receiver telling you that you were in Cleveland!

The engineers who designed the GPS system knew about these effects, of course, and the system is designed to take them into account. Some of these corrections are built into the receiver software, and some are dealt with directly. For example, the atomic clocks are deliberately set to a slower 'ticking rate' before launch to compensate for the general relativistic effects.

Thus, with the GPS, relativity has left the realm of pure theory and entered the world of engineering, and every time you use your car's navigation system you are adding to the data that verifies the theory.

LENGTH CONTRACTION AND MASS INCREASE

The experimental verification of length contraction and mass increase are not as dramatic as those verifying time dilation. The best examples involve the behavior of elementary particles in machines called synchrotrons, so we will take a moment to describe those machines.

Basically, a synchrotron is a machine whose function it is to accelerate elementary particles like protons to very high energy. This is accomplished by sending the particles into a circular vacuum chamber located inside powerful magnets. The magnetic field causes the particles to move in a circular path, and each time they pass a particular point they are accelerated by a radio frequency field. After the acceleration they are moving faster, so the magnetic field has to be increased to keep them in the vacuum chamber. This is where the name of the machine comes from—the magnetic field has to be synchronized with the particle energy.

In some machines the particle beam is brought out and allowed to collide with a target. In others, such as the Large Hadron Collider in Geneva, Switzerland, two beams circulate in opposite directions through separate vacuum systems and the beams are allowed to collide with each other head-on. (This is why they are called 'colliders'.)

The point is that the increase in mass of the particles as they speed up has to be taken into account in adjusting the magnetic field—otherwise the machine wouldn't work. Similarly, particles in synchrotrons are typically sent through in bunches, and as the speed increases the length of the bunches will decrease. This, also, has to be taken into account in maintaining the delicate synchronization of the machine. Thus, every time one of these machines works (and there are probably several operating around the world as you read this) it verifies the theory of relativity.

As we said at the start of the chapter, most of this evidence supporting relativity was accumulated after Einstein wrote his book. We can only guess at what he would have thought had he known of it.

9

GENERAL RELATIVITY AND THE EQUIVALENCE PRINCIPLE

EINSTEIN'S *RELATIVITY* CHAPTERS 18–21

> As an older friend I must advise you against [working on general relativity]... Even if you succeed, no one will believe you.
>
> Max Planck to Albert Einstein in 1913

In these chapters Einstein begins to lay the groundwork for the general theory of relativity. He concentrates on the equivalence principle—the statement that the gravitational and inertial masses are the same—to make the point that general relativity is the only way to make sense of the behavior observed in accelerated frames of reference.

At this point we have completed our discussion of special relativity and are ready to move on to the general theory. We have seen that the simple requirement that the laws of nature be the same in all inertial frames of reference led us to some unexpected conclusions about the nature of space and time, but we also saw that those conclusions are amply supported by experimental evidence. We will see the same sort of thing as we delve into general relativity. In this chapter we will address some of the preliminary issues involved in moving to the more complex theory.

As a reminder, the postulate of general relativity can be stated as follows:

> The laws of nature are the same in all frames of reference, whether or not they are accelerating.

The first questions that might occur are: What is different about systems involving acceleration? Why should they be different from inertial systems? Let's take a few moments to examine these questions.

FICTITIOUS FORCES IN NEWTONIAN PHYSICS

The main thing to realize is that accelerated frames of reference create conceptual problems in Newtonian physics, so the appearance of problems when we move to general relativity should come as no surprise. To see what I mean by this, consider a simple everyday experience—being pushed against the door of a car when the car is going around a curve at high speed. Let's examine this situation from two frames of reference—one in a spaceship far above the Earth and the other moving with the car.

From outside the car, the situation is simple. According to Newton's First Law, you will keep moving in a straight line unless acted on by a force. The car door pushes against you and makes you move in a circular path (i.e. it accelerates you). If we wanted to calculate your motion, we would simple apply Newton's Second Law which asserts the proportionality of force applied and acceleration produced, for bodies of fixed mass.

Inside the car the situation is different. You feel the door pushing against you but you are not accelerating. According to you, that is because some other force is also pushing you against the door—we call this the 'centrifugal force' (the term means 'center-fleeing'). The centrifugal force and the force provided by the door are equal in magnitude but opposite in direction. The two forces balance, so there is no unbalanced force on you and, according to Newton's First Law, you don't accelerate. (To describe this situation mathematically you would simply set the magnitude of the force exerted on you by the door equal to the magnitude of the centrifugal force.)

One important point has to be made. Although the description of events is different in the two frames of reference, the equations the two observers write down to describe their motion is exactly the same. (For reference, if F_d is the force exerted by the door, the equation is $F_d = mv^2/r$.) This is another example of the principle of relativity in operation.

Looking at these two descriptions of events, however, something jumps out at us. The observer in the spaceship does not *see* a centrifugal force acting. He or she just observes the door causing you to accelerate. You, the observer in the car, on the other hand, do experience a centrifugal force acting. We have a situation, in other words, where the existence of a force seems to depend on the frame of reference of the observer. Physicists typically refer to such forces as 'fictitious'. They seem to be something that comes up in accelerated frames of reference, but not in inertial frames. This is why we don't encounter them until we get to general relativity.

We can get further insight into the development of general relativity by considering another fictitious force, this one first understood by the French physicist and mathematician Gustave Coriolis (1792–1843). Imagine someone standing at the North Pole and throwing a ball towards someone standing on the equator. For the sake of simplicity, assume that if the Earth were not rotating the ball would follow a meridian of longitude down to the equator.

But of course, the Earth is rotating. Once more, let's describe what happens in two frames of reference—one based on a spaceship above the Earth and the other based at the point on the equator where the ball's target is standing.

An observer in the spaceship would see the ball travelling in a straight line as the Earth rotated beneath it. The rotation would carry the target along the equator, so that the ball would actually arrive at the equator to his or her left. There would be no extra forces acting in this description.

The observer on the equator sees the ball veering off to his or her left in a curved path. From Newton's First Law that observer would have to conclude that a force was acting on the ball to make it deviate from a straight-line path. In fact, this is another fictitious force. We call it the 'Coriolis force' and it explains many phenomena in our atmosphere. When you see a satellite image of a major storm, for example, you always see the clouds arranged in a swirling pattern. The clouds trace out the wind patterns, and the winds do not move in straight lines from regions of high pressure to regions of low pressure, as you might expect, because of the action of the Coriolis force. (The fact that the clouds rotate counterclockwise is due to the fact that the winds start moving in an east–west direction, rather than a north–south direction in our example.) The Coriolis force also explains why hurricanes never cross the equator, since the force acts in opposite directions on the two sides of that line.

There is a bit of folklore that holds that because of the Coriolis force the water in a flushing toilet will move in opposite directions in the northern and southern hemispheres. If the Coriolis force were the only thing influencing the water, this might be true, but it is not the only thing. In fact, experiments show that the way water enters a toilet bowl is the main determinant of the way it will leave. In effect, the water 'remembers' the way it entered for many hours, and that motion persists when the water is drained. The design of the bowl—where the exit drain is, for example— has a similar effect on the movement of the water when it leaves. Both of these effects turn out to be much stronger than the Coriolis effect. Too bad—the flushing toilets are a cute idea.

Returning to the ball thrown from the North Pole, we once again have a situation in which one observer detects a force acting and the other does not. So, Coriolis force, like centrifugal force, is, in physicist's jargon, a fictitious force.

There is another way of describing this situation, however, that may seem bizarre at first but which will start familiarizing you with the way general relativity works. Suppose the observer at the equator decided that he or she wanted to retain Newton's Laws but didn't want any fictitious forces. He or she might argue as follows: an object on which no forces act must travel in a straight line. The fact that the ball seems to curve, therefore, means that I must have the wrong definition of a straight line. Let me define a new coordinate system in which the lines from the pole to the equator follow the actual path of the ball. Let me further say that the rotation of the Earth warps the coordinate system at its surface from the familiar latitude–longitude one to the new one with curved lines. Let me call the path of the ball a 'geodesic' line. I could then describe my new situation as follows: the rotation of the Earth warps the space at its surface, and objects travel in geodesic lines in that new coordinate system.

As I said, this seems like a bizarre way to think about the Coriolis force, but in fact we will see this way of thinking again when we consider the way that general relativity deals with motion in a gravitational field.

This third way of approaching the problem of the Coriolis force also begins to illuminate the question of why it took Einstein so long to formulate his general theory. As we shall see in Chapter 11, the mathematical description of complex coordinate systems requires a type of geometry that was only developed in the nineteenth century—it's called Riemannian geometry. Furthermore, as in our example, the characteristics of the geometry are intimately connected to a physical process (the rotation of the Earth in this case). The fact that it took a man of Einstein's abilities the better part of a decade to master this geometrical system and connect it to the physical properties of the universe can be taken as testimony to the complexity of the problem.

GRAVITATIONAL AND INERTIAL MASS

There is another preliminary point we need to discuss before moving on to general relativity, and that is the nature of mass. The standard 'quick and dirty' definition says that mass is the amount of material in an object—essentially it is determined by the number of atoms. Every introductory physics course makes a point of differentiating mass and weight—an object on the moon, for example, weighs less than it does on Earth even though it has the same number of atoms. The actual definition of mass, however, is somewhat more subtle.

We can start by considering Newton's Second Law ($F = ma$). We see that in this equation, mass represents the resistance of an object to acceleration. The quantity defined in this way is called the *inertial mass*. It takes as much force to produce a given acceleration in intergalactic space as it does on the surface of the Earth, so the inertial mass of an object (unlike its weight) is the same everywhere in the universe. (Moving a heavy object on Earth will usually involve extra forces like friction, a fact which is customarily ignored in this sort of discussion.)

Having made this point, we have to say that, as was the case with time, physicists do not define what mass is, but measure it in terms of a standard. In Chapter 5, we described the international standard as the mass of a platinum-iridium block in a vault near Paris. Here's a hypothetical way you could use that block of metal and Newton's Laws to define the mass of any other object: imagine that you connected the test object to the international kilogram with a spring. If you compressed the spring and then let it go, the two masses would accelerate away from each other. Newton's Third Law says that the forces on the two masses are equal and opposite, so the ratio of the measured acceleration magnitudes will tell you the ratio of the masses. Thus, this *gedanken* experiment could be used to measure any inertial mass in terms of the international standard. (Of course, no one would actually do an experiment like this—comparisons of masses are usually made by comparing weights.)

This brings us to another way of defining mass, which depends on Newton's Law of Universal Gravitation. Recall that this law states that between any two particles in the universe there is an attractive force given by

$$F = GMm \,/\, d^2$$

where M and m are the masses of the particles, d the distance between them, and G a universal constant.

Another way of defining mass, then, is to say that it gives rise to a gravitational force. This is the *gravitational mass* of an object. The weight of an object is a measure of the interaction between the gravitational masses of the bodies involved—for an object at the surface of the Earth, for example, it is the interaction between the gravitational mass of the object and the gravitational mass of the Earth.

And this, of course, leads to a very deep question: does the gravitational mass of an object have the same value as its inertial mass? In fact, this question lies at the very core of general relativity. The statement that the two are equal is called the *equivalence principle*.

We can answer this question experimentally by considering an object with inertial mass m_i and gravitational mass m_g falling in the Earth's gravitational field. Applying Newton's Second Law to this problem yields

$$m_i a = m_g g$$

where

$$g = GM \,/\, R^2$$

and M and R are the mass and radius of the Earth, respectively. What we have called 'g' is just the magnitude of the acceleration of an object at the Earth's surface.

The point is that this equation tells us that if the principle of equivalence is true, then all objects falling in the Earth's gravitational field will experience the same acceleration. This fact was first verified experimentally by Galileo (although probably not by dropping balls from the Leaning Tower of Pisa).

Modern tests of the principle use a different technique—a technique called a torsion balance. Basically, this is a small dumbbell suspended horizontally from a wire. A large mass is brought near each end of the dumbbell, exerting a gravitational force that twists the wire. When the force exerted by the wire (which acts on the inertial mass) balances the forces exerted by the large masses (which act on the gravitational mass), the system comes to equilibrium. Scientists using high tech versions of this apparatus have verified the equivalence principle to twelve decimal places, which makes it one of the best verified statements in physics.

As we shall see in the next chapter, the equivalence principle plays a key role in the formulation of general relativity because it says that it is impossible to tell the difference between a gravitational field and the effects of a uniform acceleration. This, in turn, will explain why general relativity turns out to give us a new theory of gravity that goes beyond Newton's explanation in terms of a universal force of attraction.

THE HIGGS PARTICLE

As long as we are talking about mass, we might take a small digression to talk about a very recent advance in our understanding of this property of matter. One feature of many theories of fundamental physics has been that the question of why particles have mass, and what the masses of different particles are, is never addressed. The masses of particles are just put into the equations 'by hand', using experimentally determined numbers. We just didn't know how to deal with mass at a fundamental level of elementary particles.

In 1964, Scottish theoretical physicist Peter Higgs and a number of his colleagues realized that a solution they were proposing to resolve another problem in particle physics would also provide a resolution to this old and deep dilemma. It would, in other words, explain why particles have mass.

The basic idea is that the universe is pervaded by a field—it's called the 'Higgs field'—and different particles have different strengths of interaction with that field. It is this interaction that gives the particle its mass.

Here's a simple analogy to explain how this works: imagine a crowded city sidewalk with lots of people walking on it. Imagine also two particular people—one a large man with an armload of packages, the other an athletic and unencumbered young woman. It's clear that she will move through the crowd much more quickly than he will. Now suppose you could only see those two people, and all the others on the sidewalk were invisible to you. What would you see?

A moment's reflection will tell you that you would see the young woman moving faster. From Newton's Second Law you would conclude that she exhibited less resistance to acceleration and therefore had less mass than the man. It is clear, however, that this conclusion follows from the interactions of the man and woman with the (invisible) crowd on the sidewalk. Substitute particles for the man and the woman, and the Higgs field for the unseen crowd, and you have the modern explanation of the origin of mass.

Of course, a theory like this screams for experimental verification. It turns out that the existence of a Higgs field implies the existence of a particle known as the Higgs boson. The theory predicted that this particle would be very massive—perhaps even more than a hundred times more massive than the proton. To produce a particle of this mass would require a great deal of energy, and this, in turn, meant that the discovery of the particle had to wait until a machine capable of reaching these sorts of energies became available.

In Chapter 8 we described the operation of synchrotrons and colliders. The most powerful machine in the world today is the Large Hadron Collider (LHC), operated by the European Center for Nuclear Research (CERN) just outside of Geneva, Switzerland. In this machine—arguably the most technologically sophisticated apparatus ever built—beams of protons circulate in opposite directions as they are accelerated, then collide head on. For a brief instant in a volume the size of a proton, scientists can re-create the conditions that existed when the universe was a fraction of a second old. In July 2013, CERN scientists announced conclusive evidence that they had seen the Higgs particle in the debris of LHC collisions. The particle weighed in at about 125 times the mass of the proton. By a fortunate stroke of luck, Peter Higgs himself was in the audience to hear the confirmation of a prediction he had made almost fifty years earlier. He shared the 2013 Nobel Prize in Physics for this work.

One final point. In 1993, physicist Leon Lederman and science journalist Dick Teresi wrote a popular book about the state of particle physics. Somewhere along the line in the production process, the book's title became *The God Particle* (a reference to the Higgs boson). The name really caught on in the popular press and figured prominently in media reports of the discovery of the particle. Some physicists profess to find the term embarrassing and it is certainly not used much inside the physics community. For myself, my experience is that authors often have surprisingly little input into the process of finding a name for their books—such decisions are often driven more by marketing strategies than anything else. In any case, I think the 'God Particle' will be with us for a long time.

10

GENERAL RELATIVITY AND GRAVITY

EINSTEIN'S *RELATIVITY* CHAPTER 22

Anyone who is not bothered [by quantum mechanics] must have rocks in his head.

Attributed to physicist David Mermin

In this chapter Einstein lays out a qualitative argument that gravity may be an effect seen by observers in accelerated reference frames, and therefore may be described by general relativity.

Before we get into the technical details of general relativity, it would probably be a good idea to look at some general intuitive arguments that underlie the theory. Writing in the 1930s, Einstein used the analogy of a man in an elevator to carry out this task. Today, we can take advantage of modern technology and talk about an observer in a ship in intergalactic space where, to all intents and purposes, there is no gravitational field. Our goal will be to understand why the equivalence principle, together with the postulate of general relativity, leads us to a new understanding of gravity. We will then take a brief excursion into quantum mechanics to see why this new understanding creates a deep and fundamental problem in physics.

Before we climb into our spaceship, however, let's look at a mundane example to convince ourselves that the association of gravity and acceleration is not unreasonable. Think about the last time you were in an elevator in a tall building. When the elevator starts up, there is a moment when you feel you are being pressed into the floor. Similarly, when you start down, there is a momentary sensation of floating. If you took a bathroom scale into the elevator (as I once did in the Sears Tower in Chicago) you would note that the number on the scale would increase slightly when you start up and decrease slightly when you start down. It also would read normally once the elevator had reached its (constant) operating speed. Whatever it is that is being registered on the scale seems to be affected by the acceleration of the elevator cage. The fact that the scale reads normally once the acceleration is over and the elevator is moving at a constant speed tells us that whatever those effects are, they do not show up in inertial systems. Since we normally associate the reading on a scale with weight, and weight results from the gravitational attraction of the Earth, this simple everyday example suggests that considering *frames of reference* incorporating acceleration will give us insights into the force of gravity.

Now let's move our operation into that ship in intergalactic space and think about a few simple experiments. As usual, we will examine each experiment from two frames of reference—one in the ship, the other a non-accelerating frame outside of it.

Let's start with the ship moving at a constant velocity (constant speed v in a fixed direction), and let's suppose the observer in the ship has a ball. He or she holds the ball out and lets it go. What happens?

To an observer outside the ship, the observer in the ship and the ball are both moving with constant velocity; so, according to Newton's First Law, the ball will keep moving at speed v and stay even with that person's hand. The observer on the ship thinks that he or she is stationary, and will interpret the fact that the ball doesn't fall as being due to the absence of gravity.

Incidentally, the 'weightlessness' you have seen in films taken on the Space Shuttle or the International Space Station does not result from the absence of gravity. The Earth's gravitational field at its surface, 4000 miles from its center, and at the Shuttle orbit, 4000 plus 100 miles or so, is about the same. The apparent weightlessness in the shuttle arises because, in the frame of the Shuttle, gravity is canceled out by centrifugal force.

Now let's change the experiment. Let the spaceship be accelerating with an acceleration of magnitude a, and let the observer in the spaceship be standing on a scale. What happens?

First we have to understand how a scale works. A simple picture to have in mind is that a scale is simply a platform mounted on a spring. When an object is placed on the platform it exerts a downward force of the same magnitude as its weight. This causes the spring to compress and exert an upward force. Equilibrium is reached when the upward force exerted by the spring has the same magnitude as the downward force of the object's weight. The amount of compression of the spring is measured and displayed as the 'weight' of the object.

The observer outside of the spaceship sees a scenario in which the ship is being accelerated, and is consequently pushing the scale up against the feet of the observer in the ship. The scale then exerts a force that causes the spaceship observer to accelerate along with the ship. The force acts on the inertial mass of the spaceship observer.

The observer in the spaceship does not feel that he or she is accelerating, but feels a force pushing him or her down into the scale. He or she would conclude that there was a gravitational force acting, and that force would, of course, act on the observer's gravitational mass, which, according to the equivalence principle, is the same as the inertial mass.

Just as was the case with the centrifugal and Coriolis forces we discussed in the last chapter, then, we have a situation where the presence of a force seems to depend on the frame of reference—it's there in one frame and not in another. Provided that the equivalence principle holds, however, both observers will write down the same equation to describe the situation. The question then becomes this: is gravity another fictitious force?

Let's look at another little experiment to explore this question. Suppose, while the spaceship is accelerating, the observer holds the ball out again and lets it go. What happens?

For the outside observer, once the ball is released it will keep moving at whatever velocity it had at the time it was let go. The ship, meanwhile, is accelerating, and eventually the floor will move up until it contacts the ball. After this happens, the floor will exert a force on the ball and make it accelerate at the same rate as the ship.

The observer on the ship, however, observes the ball move downward and hit the floor. In other words, he or she will observe the effect of a gravitational force pulling the ball down. Once again, one observer detects a gravitational force acting, the other does not.

One way of making the point that gravity is a fictitious force is to note that if there were no windows on the spaceship, the observer inside would have no way of determining if he or she were on Earth (i.e. in the Earth's gravitational field) or in a ship in intergalactic space accelerating at the rate we called 'g' (32 feet/sec/sec or 9.8 m/sec/sec). As we will discuss shortly, this makes gravity a strange kind of force, a force different from the other kinds of forces that operate in the universe.

Before going into that, however, let's consider a few more simple experiments in our accelerating spaceship. Suppose the observer makes a mark on the wall and throws a ball at it. As above, the outside observer will see the ship move up as the ball flies, so that the ball will hit below the mark. The observer in the ship, on the other hand, will claim there is a force pulling the ball down and attribute the deviation to gravity. Simple enough.

Now suppose that instead of throwing the ball the observer in the spaceship shines a flashlight at the wall. By the reasoning in the previous paragraph, the beam will hit below the mark, just as the ball did. And this, in turn, leads us to our first prediction based on the postulate of general relativity: the path of light beams will be deflected in a gravitational field. We will discuss the details of this prediction and its verification in Chapter 13, but here we simply note that it was the verification of this prediction that led to the sudden fame that Einstein experienced, as discussed in Chapter 1. It is important to understand that although we have come to this result using the analogy of the spaceship, the bending of light is a prediction of general relativity and does not depend on that spaceship in any way.

GRAVITY AS ODD MAN OUT

The above arguments show that gravity is a phenomenon that is intimately connected to coordinate systems and geometry, a point we will make in more detail in the next chapter. Before we do that, however, I would like to make a slight digression to explore the modern understanding of the nature of force in general and compare that with our understanding of gravity to describe what is perhaps the deepest unsolved problem in fundamental physics—our inability to reconcile the two great revolutionary scientific advances of the twentieth century: general relativity and quantum mechanics.

The word 'quantum' comes from the Latin for 'heap' or 'bundle', and 'mechanics' is the traditional word for the science of force and motion. Thus, quantum mechanics is the study of the motion of things that come in bundles. In the world inside the atom, matter comes in bundles we call particles, and it turns out that everything else—energy, momentum, charge, spin, and so on—comes in bundles as well. This is a strange world, full of seemingly incomprehensible notions, but it is the development of quantum mechanics that led (among other things) to the modern information revolution. Strange as it seems to us, quantum mechanics really does describe the world of the atom.

The quantum picture of force was first suggested by the Japanese physicist Hideki Yukawa in 1935. It depends on something called the Heisenberg Uncertainty Principle, named after the German physicist Werner Heisenberg (1901–1976), one of the founders of quantum mechanics. The version of the principle we want to use can be stated in this way: the uncertainty in our knowledge of the energy of a system multiplied by the uncertainty in the time at which the system had that energy has to be greater than a quantity called the Planck constant. In equation form

$$\Delta E \times \Delta t \geq h / 2\pi$$

where the Greek letter delta (Δ) represents the amount of uncertainty and h, Plank's constant, is a physical quantity, measured in units known as joule seconds, that has a numerical value of about 6.6×10^{-34}.

This equation tells us that if we want to know the energy of a system exactly (i.e. if we want ΔE to be zero) then the time at which the system had that energy has to be completely unknown (i.e. Δt has to be infinite) and vice versa. The equation also tells us that the energy of a system can fluctuate (i.e. ΔE can have some non-zero value) for a short time (i.e. for a small Δt).

But we know from $E = mc^2$ that a fluctuation in energy corresponds to a fluctuation in mass, which means that the Uncertainty Principle implies that extra particles can appear in a system, provided that they disappear in a time less than Δt. Like Cinderella at the ball, so long as they don't stay too long, these so-called 'virtual' particles can pop up and play a role in the interaction between ordinary particles before they disappear. This is just one of the strange results predicted by quantum mechanics and is, like many quantum mechanical processes, extremely counter-intuitive. Nevertheless, although we don't have space here to go into it, the existence of virtual particles has been well verified experimentally.

What Yukawa realized was that a virtual particle whose mass was greater than the electron's but less than the proton's could last long enough to travel across an atomic nucleus. As we mentioned in Chapter 8, he called this particle a 'meson' ('intermediate one')—today it's called a pion (pronounced 'PIE-on') and denoted by the Greek letter 'pi' (π). The particle was first seen in the debris of cosmic ray collisions in 1947.

Yukawa suggested that the strong force—the fundamental interaction that holds the nucleus together—was generated by the exchange of virtual pions between protons and neutrons in the nucleus. The idea that forces have their fundamental origin in this quantum mechanical effect has become one of the cornerstones of modern physics (Yukawa received the Nobel Prize for this work in 1949).

The basic idea is this: as allowed by the Uncerainty Principle, a particle in the nucleus emits a short-lived virtual particle, and that virtual particle lives just long enough to carry energy and momentum to another particle that absorbs it. The exchange of virtual particles thus generates a 'force' between the two non-virtual particles. (We are using the term 'force' just to indicate an interaction that transfers energy and momentum.)

Recall that physicists recognize four fundamental forces (or interactions) in nature: the strong force, which holds the nucleus together; the familiar electromagnetic force; the weak force, which governs some types of radioactive decay; and gravity. Of these, we have well verified theories that describe the first three in terms of the exchange of virtual particles. The forces differ from each other because they are generated by the exchange of different kinds of virtual particles. For example, the electromagnetic force is generated by the exchange of photons (see Chapter 1), so the force that allows a magnet to hold up a piece of metal is actually generated by a flood of virtual photons being exchanged between particles in the metal and atoms in the magnet. Similarly, the weak force is generated by the exchange of heavy particles designated by the letters W and Z. The strong force can be discussed at two levels. In Yukawa's theory, the exchange of mesons between what were then called elementary particles generates the force that holds them together. Today we realize that these so-called 'elementary' particles are actually made of things more elementary still—things called 'quarks'. At this level, the more fundamental level, the strong force is generated by the exchange of particles called 'gluons' (because they 'glue' the quarks together). The prosaically named 'Standard Model' is a very successful quantum theory which describes all three of these forces in terms of the exchange of virtual particles.

But not gravity. Despite the heroic efforts of an entire generation of brilliant theoretical physicists, we still do not have a generally accepted theory that describes the gravitational force in quantum terms. In Chapter 14 we'll describe some modern attempts to fill this gap, but for the moment general relativity, with its stubborn reliance on geometrical effects instead of virtual particle exchange, remains our best theory of gravitation. It is to this theory that we now turn.

11

THE FORMULATION OF GENERAL RELATIVITY
EINSTEIN'S *RELATIVITY*
CHAPTERS 23–29

Whenever I have to explain a theorem in multiple dimensions, I keep a 3×5 card in my pocket showing how it works in two.

Mathematician Menahem Schiffer

In these chapters Einstein lays out the geometrical underpinnings of general relativity. He starts by talking about clocks and measuring rods in rotating systems and then moves on to discuss the so-called Gaussian coordinates and presents a formulation of the theory.

COORDINATES

In Chapter 3 we introduced the notion of a coordinate system and discussed Cartesian coordinates. So long as we confined our attention to inertial frames, we didn't have to go any farther in that discussion. As we saw in our discussion of the Coriolis force in Chapter 10, however, the use of accelerated frames of reference introduces the possibility that we may need a more general kind of coordinate system in general relativity. We will, therefore, make a slight diversion here to talk about some nineteenth-century developments in mathematics.

Johann Carl Frederick Gauss (1777–1855) is generally regarded as one of the greatest (if not *the* greatest) mathematicians who ever lived. He was born into a poor family in Brunswick in what is now Germany, but was such a prodigy that the Duke of Brunswick sent him to the university. To recount just one story of his youth, it happened that his mother, who was illiterate, did not record his birth, but remembered that it happened eight days before the Feast of the Ascension, which occurs forty days after Easter. As a young man in 1800, Gauss worked out a system for calculating when Easter would fall in any year, and thereby determined his own birthday. (This is not a trivial problem, since Easter is tied to the Jewish celebration of Passover, whose date is fixed in the lunar calendar.)

Among his many accomplishments, Gauss laid the groundwork for what would become the geometrical underpinnings of general relativity. He spent some time as a surveyor, and was interested in the geometry of two-dimensional surfaces embedded in a three-dimensional space (think hills and valleys).

To understand his conclusions, let's start by thinking about two points in an ordinary Cartesian plane. Let ds be the straight line distance between these points, and let dx and dy be the differences between their x and y coordinates, respectively. (The use of the 'd' is customary and indicates that the distances involved are infinitesimally small.) Then from the Pythagorean Theorem

$$ds^2 = dx^2 + dy^2$$

This distance represents the shortest path between the two points—what we called a geodesic in the last chapter. Note that this distance will not change if we rotate the coordinate system or make other kinds of changes.

Now let's imagine a convoluted two-dimensional surface on top of this plane—a series of hills and valleys. If you were constrained to move on that surface, as Gauss was when he was a surveyor, you would have to work with a coordinate system on a surface that wasn't a plane. Gauss defined such a coordinate system by laying a grid over the convoluted surface. (Einstein labels the new coordinates u and v, shows such a system in Fig. 4, and refers to the new curved surface as a 'mollusk'.) In terms of these new coordinates, the distance between two points will be given by

$$ds^2 = g_{11}du^2 + g_{22}dv^2 + g_{12}du\ dv$$

where, as before, du and dv are the (infinitesimally) small distances between points on the convoluted surface. The expressions labeled 'g' are elements of what is called a metric tensor. They are (generally complicated) mathematical expressions that depend on the curvature of the surface at any point in space.

Note that when the surface is a plane and the coordinates are the familiar Cartesian coordinates (so $du = dx$ and $dv = dy$), the expressions for the metric tensor reduce to

$$g_{11} = g_{22} = 1$$

and

$$g_{12} = 0$$

as expressed above for a Cartesian system.

In general, there are many possible paths we could take between neighboring points. To find the shortest path—what we have called the geodesic—a branch of mathematics called the calculus of variations is used. Although the details of this kind of calculation are beyond the scope of this book, you can get some idea of how it works by thinking about the distance between two points on the surface of the Earth—take New York and London as examples. There are many paths an airplane might take between these two cities—over the North Pole, down to the tropics, and so on. The calculus of variations shows that the shortest of these paths is the shorter arc of a great circle that passes between New York and London, which explains why flights between those cities occasionally pass over parts of Greenland.

In 1854, the German mathematician Bernhard Riemann (1826–1866) published a lecture titled 'On the Hypotheses on which Geometry is Based.' This work extended Gauss' system to geometries with an arbitrary number of dimensions, and, since we already know that relativity demands a four-dimensional space-time (three spatial dimensions plus time), Riemannian geometry becomes the framework on which the theory is built. The fact that these dimensions interchange with each other when viewed from different frames of reference explains the standard use of the term 'space-time' in describing coordinate systems in general relativity.

Riemann actually made many fundamental contributions to mathematics in his tragically short life. It is a tribute to the breadth of his work that his contribution to relativity is often mentioned almost as an afterthought in his biographies.

GENERAL RELATIVITY

With our basic geometrical system in place, we can now proceed to a discussion of the theory of general relativity itself. As we have said, the principle behind the theory can be stated as:

The laws of nature are the same in all frames of reference.

where, as Einstein stresses, the frames of reference now refer to all Gaussian coordinate systems.

Although the actual working out of the mathematical consequences of this statement is beyond the scope of this book, we can nonetheless summarize the general ideas behind the theory in the following two statements:

The presence of matter and radiation distorts the space-time grid.

and

Matter and radiation move along geodesics in the distorted space-time grid.

Note that this distortion of the space-time grid is analogous to the distortion of the Earth's coordinate system we discussed in conjunction with the Coriolis force in Chapter 9.

There is a simple two-dimensional analogy that illustrates how the theory works. Imagine a flexible plastic sheet stretched taut and marked out in a standard Cartesian grid. Now imagine dropping a heavy weight—a bowling ball, for example—on that sheet. The weight will distort the sheet, so that instead of a flat plane it now has a depression in its center. We can say that the grid is distorted by the presence of the bowling ball.

Now imagine shooting a marble across the sheet. If the marble come near the bowling ball, it will enter the depression and have its direction of motion changed. It goes into the depression moving in one direction and exits moving in another. How would this event be described by different observers?

A Newtonian observer would see the direction of motion change and, according to the First Law of Motion, say that a force had acted on the marble. That observer, in fact, would describe this force as the mutual gravitational attraction between the ball and the marble and invoke the Law of Universal Gravitation to explain the change in direction. This observer, in other words, would give a dynamical interpretation of events.

A relativistic observer, on the other hand, would give a very different description. This observer would say that the presence of the bowling ball distorted the space-time grid, and that the marble was simply following the geodesic in the new system. He or she, in other words, would give a geometrical interpretation of what happened. In his or her world, there would be no forces, only geometry.

This difference in interpretation is simply another illustration of the issue we raised earlier: the description of gravity given by general relativity is fundamentally different from the description of the other three fundamental interactions in nature. Nevertheless, general relativity remains our best and most reliable theory of gravitation, and healing this split between the fundamental interactions remains a major goal in theoretical physics—a point to which we will return in Chapter 14. Before that, however, we need to take a look at the experimental tests of general relativity, which have advanced quite a bit since Einstein's time.

12

EXPERIMENTAL TESTS OF GENERAL RELATIVITY
EINSTEIN'S *RELATIVITY* CHAPTERS 28–29, APPENDIX 3

Another beautiful theory killed by an ugly fact.

J.B.S. Haldane

When Einstein wrote his book there was very little experimental evidence to test general relativity—a situation that has changed considerably since then. He discusses what have come to be called the 'classical' tests of the theory.

No scientific theory can be accepted unless it meets the ultimate test—do its predictions match nature? Obviously, a theory that makes a prediction that is patently wrong needs to be modified or replaced, but there is a more subtle question we can ask: how much confirmation does a theory have to have before it is generally accepted?

The answer to this question varies from situation to situation. The reason for this is that the judgment of the scientific community depends on many things beside data. The data has to be there, of course, but once it is, many other factors come into play. In our discussion of general relativity we will look at only one of these factors—beauty.

It may seem strange to talk of a quality like beauty in a discussion of a scientific theory, but it does have an influence on acceptance. Basically, if a theory is beautiful and elegant (as general relativity surely is) scientists are willing to accept it when it is supported by less copious data than when it isn't. For example, it required massive amounts of data from all over the world to drive the geological community to accept the theory of plate tectonics, our best theory of the operation of the Earth. General relativity, as we shall see below, was accepted early on because of two pieces of data. Thus, we can think of a quality like beauty as being involved in setting the bar on the acceptance of a theory—the more beautiful the theory is, the less data is needed for acceptance.

Having said this, I have to emphasize again that the data has to be there before considerations of beauty can be brought into play. This is encapsulated in the quote by the British biologist J.B.S. Haldane that opens this chapter.

All of which brings us to the question of how well general relativity is supported by experimental evidence. As was the case with special relativity, general relativity reduces to the ordinary Newtonian picture when it is applied to normal-sized objects moving at normal speeds. This means that to test the theory we will have to find places where it produces predictions that differ from those of Newtonian physics, and this, in turn, means that we will either have to look for situations where there is a high concentration of matter or radiation (and hence a measureable warping of the space-time grid), or make very accurate measurements.

The experimental tests of the theory can be broken down into two sets—the so-called classical tests (those available in the early twentieth century) and the modern ones. We'll look at these two categories separately.

CLASSICAL TESTS

There are three tests that are generally considered to be in this category: the perihelion shift of mercury, the bending of light by the sun, and the gravitational redshift of light. Of these, only the first two were available in the 1930s, when Einstein wrote his book.

PERIHELION SHIFT

Kepler showed that a single planet circling a star will move in an elliptical orbit, and that that orbit will not change over time. In the solar system, however, the planets all exert (small) gravitational influences on each other, and this has an effect on their orbits. Basically, it makes the orbital ellipse rotate slowly, so that the point at which the planet is closest to the sun (the so-called perihelion) moves farther along with each orbit. This effect is called the 'advance of the perihelion'.

It's not a big effect. Because of its proximity to the sun, Mercury has the biggest perihelion advance, and it is only 5600 arcseconds (about a degree and a half) per century. As small as this effect is, it was easily measured by nineteenth-century astronomers. Newtonian calculations, based on the gravitational attraction of the other planets, could account for 5557 arcseconds per century, but that left 43 arcseconds per century unaccounted for. Einstein was able to show that general relativity predicted precisely this amount of perihelion shift, and this was the first experimental triumph of the theory.

I should point out that this is not, strictly speaking, the experimental verification of a theoretical prediction. Instead, it is the explanation of a previously unexplained result. Scientists call such a result a 'retrodiction'.

Using modern techniques, scientists since Einstein have determined the advance of the perihelion for several planets—the relativistic effect for Venus is 8.62 arcseconds per century, for Earth 3.84 arcseconds per century, and for Mars 1.35 arcseconds per century, for example. All of these are consistent with the predictions of the theory.

BENDING OF LIGHT

In Chapter 10 we presented an intuitive argument as to why we might expect light to be deflected by gravitation based on the principle of equivalence. In fact, like the marble rolling across the distorted grid in Chapter 11, light passing near a massive object will be deflected from its original course. In particular, light from a star passing near the sun will appear to be coming to Earth from a slightly different angle than light from that same source at another time of year, when it comes to Earth directly without passing near the sun. The problem with this statement, of course, is that when a star is located in a position where its light passes near the sun, that light is completely blotted out by light from the sun itself. In the early twentieth century the only way around this problem was to wait for an eclipse of the sun. The idea was to photograph a star field when it was above the horizon at night, then wait several months and photograph the same star field during a total eclipse of the sun.

An opportunity to test this prediction arose in May 1919, when an expedition led by (later Sir) Arthur Eddington photographed star fields during an eclipse from the island of Principe in West Africa. (The event was also photographed from a location in Brazil.) It was the confirmation of general relativity from this expedition that led to Einstein's sudden vault to fame that we described in Chapter 1.

There is a minor scholarly debate about how accurate Eddington's results actually were. By modern standards, the quality of his measurements were indeed poor, and the results from the Brazilian part of the expedition were pretty ambiguous. Nevertheless, modern astronomers who have re-examined Eddington's data have confirmed his conclusions. In any case, the results were quickly verified by astronomers at Lick Observatory in California in 1922.

Today, bending-of-light experiments are done with radio waves from distant quasars. This technique has the enormous advantage that it can be done in broad daylight, without the need of an eclipse, since the sun is a weak radio source that doesn't obscure the quasars. There is no doubt today that Einstein's prediction of the bending of electromagnetic radiation by massive objects is well verified.

GRAVITATIONAL RED SHIFT

The third classical test of relativity wasn't actually carried out until 1959, so it did not play a role in the early acceptance of the theory. General relativity predicts that light moving upward in a gravitational field will lose energy. Since the light must always travel at a speed c, this means that its frequency will shift towards the red. By the same token, light falling in a gravitational field will be shifted towards the blue (i.e. higher energy). (Technically, we should point out that this prediction can be derived from the equivalence principle, so it doesn't test the full theory of relativity.)

The experimental problem can be stated quite simply. If you shoot a light beam straight up from the surface of the Earth to the top of a 100-foot tower, the prediction is that the frequencies measured at the top and bottom will differ only in the *fifteenth* decimal place! This means that if you can't determine the actual frequency to something close to this accuracy, you won't be able to tell the difference between the light at the top and bottom of the tower, and hence won't be able to test Einstein's prediction.

Atoms emit light when electrons jump from one orbit to another. When you look at the light given off by a collection of atoms, however, some emitting atoms are moving toward you and some away from you. This changes the frequencies of light you get from different atoms. In addition, when atoms emit light, they recoil, just as a gun recoils when it 'emits' a bullet, and this, too, changes the frequency you measure. In the end, these effects (and many others) smear out the frequency of the light. Instead of detecting a single frequency, you find a range of frequencies spread out in a bell curve. If the width of that bell curve is too big, it will hide the small gravitational red shift associated with general relativity.

Today, of course, we use lasers to produce well-defined frequencies of light, so these problems are no longer important. Back in 1959, however, the laser wasn't invented, and some other scheme had to be found to reduce the width of the bell curve. Two American physicists at Harvard, Robert Pound and his then graduate student Glen Rebka, realized that a newly discovered phenomenon could be used to do this. Called the Mossbauer effect (after its discoverer, German physicist Rudolph Mossbauer), it allowed certain solids, under the right conditions, to emit extremely precise frequencies of light. Basically, in these solids the recoil of the emitting atom is shared out among all the atoms in the system, and this greatly reduces the recoil and the width of the bell curve. Using this effect, Pound and Rebka carried out the experiment and found that they could produce bell curves 'only' 100 times wider than the expected difference in frequency between the top and bottom of their apparatus. With some experimental and data analysis tricks, this allowed them to detect the gravitational red shift for the first time.

This story illustrates an important point about science. Sometimes answers to the deepest questions (in this case, the nature of space-time) depend on the grubbiest details of experimental technique (like measuring the frequency of a light beam).

The Pound–Rebka experiment represents something of a turning point in the testing of general relativity. It was the last of the 'classical' tests of the theory, and it opened the way for the new generation of high precision tests that were to follow.

MODERN TESTS

There are several categories of modern tests of the theory. One category, like the use of quasars to measure the bending of electromagnetic radiation by the sun, involves the use of modern techniques to refine the classical tests. We have already given a brief discussion of some of these above. Another category involves testing the same principles involved in the classical tests (the bending of light, for example) but in new situations. Finally, there are tests that involve situations not dealt with in the classical tests.

Before we get into a discussion of the last two categories, we should note that in Chapter 8 we talked about what is to my mind the most striking test of relativity—the role it plays in the global positioning system. In that chapter we saw that signals from the system's satellites have to be corrected for both special and general relativistic effects. Thus, every time someone turns on the navigational system in his or her car—an event that must happen millions of times a day—we have another experimental verification of general relativity.

TIME DELAY EXPERIMENTS

This class of experiments is another way of measuring the effect of gravitational fields on light. First suggested by Harvard astronomer Irwin Shapiro, the basic idea is to bounce a radar signal from a planet as it is about to disappear behind the sun or to re-appear on the other side. The radar signal is just another kind of electromagnetic radiation, so when it passes near the sun it will be affected by the warping of the space-time grid. This will produce a measurable delay in the time it takes the signal to get back to Earth. In the 1970s, such experiments verified general relativity at the level of 5 percent uncertainty, a number that has since been reduced to 0.1 percent.

More recently, in 2003 Italian scientists took advantage of a chance alignment of the Cassini spacecraft (which was then on its way to Saturn) to repeat the experiment at a much higher level of accuracy. Measuring the radio signal passing near the sun while going to and returning from the space probe allowed them to claim a confirmation of general relativity at the level of 0.002 percent uncertainty—a high level of accuracy indeed.

GRAVITATIONAL LENSING

To understand gravitational lensing, you should picture three things: a distant galaxy which is the source of a light signal, an observer on Earth, and, between these two, another massive object like a galaxy. As light from the source passes near the intermediate mass, its direction will be changed by the warped space-time grid. Thus these light beams will come to the Earth from a different direction than they would have otherwise, and the observer will see the position of the light source displaced from what it actually is. In effect, the intermediate mass acts as a kind of lens to focus the light.

Einstein had suggested that such an effect might be seen early on, but this prediction wasn't verified until 1979. Astronomers then saw what looked to be two separate quasars whose time variations seemed to be exactly the same. They eventually realized that what they were seeing was one quasar whose light was passing both above and below an intermediate galaxy, creating a twin image.

If the source, intermediate mass, and observer are lined up exactly, the observer will see a ring of light (it's called an 'Einstein ring'). If the alignment is a little off, the observer will see arcs. Such displays are common in the sky.

Like many other areas of relativity, gravitational lensing has gone from being a test of the theory to being a tool for other investigations. Today, it is one way that astronomers look for unseen concentrations of non-luminous matter in the universe.

FRAME DRAGGING AND THE GEODETIC EFFECT

In the Newtonian world the gravitational field of the Earth depends only on its mass—the fact that the Earth is rotating has nothing to do with any gravitational effect. Early on in the development of general relativity it was realized that rotation would affect the way a massive object interacted with the space-time grid. The standard analogy to illustrate this is to imagine spinning something like a basketball in a vat of molasses. The rotating ball will pull some of the molasses along with it, causing the fluid to rotate. In the same way, the rotation of the Earth drags the space-time grid along with it, an effect called frame dragging.

There is another effect associated with rotation in general relativity. A spinning object in orbit around a massive object would exhibit a small change in the direction of its axis of rotation because of the warping of the space-time grid by the large object. (You can think of this as being due to the spinning object 'leaning in' as it circles in the warped grid.) This is called the 'geodetic effect'. In 1959, Stanford physicist Leonard Schiff (1915–1971) pointed out that a gyroscope in orbit around the Earth could test two predictions of general relativity—frame dragging and the geodetic effect. Neither of these were included in the classical tests outlined above.

One test of frame dragging was done using the LAGEOS satellites (the acronym stands for Laser Geodynamic Satellite), which are basically laser reflectors in long-term stable Earth orbits. By far the most interesting story, though, concerns a mission known as Gravity Probe B. This experiment began at Stanford University in the 1960s as an attempt to test the two predictions mentioned above. Physicist Francis Everitt took over the project, which was technologically daunting. The idea was to put a set of extremely stable gyroscopes into orbit and measure the tiny changes in their rotation caused by relativistic effects. One interesting outcome of the work was the production of what were called the 'world's roundest objects'—ping pong ball sized quartz spheres that, had they been blown up to the size of the Earth, would have their highest 'mountain' be only a few feet high.

The project just seemed to drag on as Everitt and his team dealt with one technical difficulty after another. In addition, the project was at the mercy of NASA's launch schedule, and was delayed by events like the *Challenger* disaster in 1986. Throughout the 1990s, a kind of pessimism about the enterprise seemed to develop—I can remember being at NASA planning meetings, for example, in which senior administrators talked openly about trying to kill the project. There must have been a feeling of relief at Stanford when the project was actually put into orbit in 2004. After about a year and a half of data collecting and several years of analysis, the project team announced that both the geodetic and frame dragging effects had been seen and were consistent with the predictions of general relativity.

Unfortunately, by the time these results came in, high precision tests of both of these effects had been made (by measuring light signals moving with and against the Earth's rotation, for example), so in the end the results from Gravity Probe B were less important than they might have been.

Incidentally, Gravity Probe A was a sounding rocket launched in 1976 that confirmed Einstein's prediction that clocks at higher altitude would run faster than clocks on the ground.

GRAVITATIONAL WAVES

In Maxwell's electromagnetic theory, when a charge is accelerated, it gives off electromagnetic radiation. It turns out that an analogous process occurs in general relativity. When a mass is accelerated, it sets up an outgoing ripple in the space-time grid, something like the ripple on a pond surface when a rock is thrown in. These so-called gravitational waves are actually more complicated than either of these analogies might suggest, however. If you imagine a sphere like a basketball, for example, it will be distorted as a gravitational wave goes by. First it will be distorted into an ellipse with the long axis in the one direction, then into an ellipse with its long axis in the perpendicular direction, then back again. It will continue the alternate stretching and compressing process until the wave has gone by and it reverts to its original spherical shape.

As we have mentioned, the existence of gravitational waves is predicted by general relativity. As of this writing, however, we have no direct evidence of their existence—a point to which we will return in Chapter 14. We do, however, have some very strong indirect evidence.

In 1974, astronomer Joseph Taylor and Russell Hulse, working at the radio telescope in Arecibo, Puerto Rico, discovered and analyzed an amazing object in the sky. Dubbed PSR 1913+16, it was two pulsars circling each other in close orbit. A pulsar is the end state of massive stars. Typically a pulsar is about ten miles across and composed almost entirely of neutrons—think of it as an oversized atomic nucleus. Pulsars rotate rapidly and send out radio beams along their axis of rotation, so that if you are standing in the beam you will see a pulse every time it sweeps by—this is where the name 'pulsar' comes from.

The regular pulsing allows astronomers to make very accurate measurements of the motion of the pulsar. In this case, they quickly realized that they had found a truly unusual object—two neutron stars orbiting each other every eight hours. Given the intensely strong gravitational fields in such a system, it was a perfect place to look for the effects of general relativity. For example, the advance of the perihelion (actually, 'periastrion' is a more appropriate word) is about 4 degrees per year—many orders of magnitude greater than that found for Mercury.

The most important thing about the system, however, is that the two stars are spiraling in toward each other at the rate of about 1 cm/day. Calculations of all the forces operating in the system can explain this result only if the system is losing energy by radiating away gravitational waves. In this case, the books balance. For this work, Hulse and Taylor received the Nobel Prize in 1993.

More recently, in 2013, astronomers found another unusual object—a pulsar orbiting a white dwarf (another possible end state for a star—a star about the size of the Earth). In this system the two companion stars circle each other about every two and a half hours and, once again, the details of the orbit can only be explained if gravitational waves are being emitted.

We will turn to the attempt to measure gravitational waves directly in Chapter 14.

13

COSMOLOGY

EINSTEIN'S *RELATIVITY*
CHAPTERS 30–32

Once we too beyond the veil have passed
Oh, but the long, long time the world shall last.

Rubaiyat of Omar Khayam

Einstein spends most of his time in these chapters arguing that the universe can be finite in size and still unbounded, but this is not considered to be a major issue among cosmologists today.

Of all the fields of science that were being pursued in the 1930s, when Einstein was writing his book, few have seen as much development as cosmology, the study of the large-scale structure and dynamics of the universe. To take just one example among many, it wasn't so long ago that cosmologists were having serious debates about whether the age of the universe was 7 billion or 20 billion years. Earlier, there was even an embarrassing (though mercifully shortlived) period when the age of the universe as calculated by cosmologists was actually less than the age of the Earth! Today, thanks to the massive improvement in observational techniques over the last generation, that same age is confidently reported to be 13.798 billion years, with an uncertainty of 0.037 billion years. In this chapter, then, we will present a short sketch of the state of cosmology today, emphasizing the continued importance of Einstein's work in general relativity.

EDWIN HUBBLE AND THE BIG BANG

In a real sense, we can say that modern observational cosmology began in the late 1920s, with the work of the American astronomer Edwin Hubble (1889–1953). Hubble had an interesting life, having been a Rhodes Scholar at Oxford and practiced law before taking his PhD from the University of Chicago and enlisting in the army in World War I (he eventually became a major in the infantry). In 1919 he was offered a position at the Mount Wilson Observatory outside of Los Angeles, which was then the site of the world's largest telescope. It was at Mount Wilson that Hubble made the observations that established our modern picture of the universe.

At the turn of the last century there was a major debate among astronomers about the nature of certain objects that could be seen in the sky. Called nebulae (from the Latin for 'cloud'), these were fuzzy patches of luminous material whose internal structure couldn't be resolved with the telescopes available at the time. The question at issue was whether the nebulae were simply structures within the Milky Way or were, in the marvelous phrase introduced by Immanuel Kant, other 'island universes' (what we would call galaxies today).

The point is that we can imagine many different kinds of universes— one with stars scattered everywhere, another with all the stars in one central clump, and another populated by galaxies. Choosing between these possibilities is the job of the observational astronomer, and that's where Edwin Hubble and the Mount Wilson telescope came in. The new telescope was able to identify individual stars in the nebulae, and, as we shall see, this allowed Hubble to determine how far away they are.

In the late nineteenth century the Harvard astronomer Henrietta Leavitt (1868–1921) had developed a way of determining the distance to a certain class of stars known as Cepheid variables (the name comes from the fact that the first star of this type was seen in the constellation Cepheus, which is visible in the northern hemisphere). These stars go through a regular cycle of brightening and dimming over a period of weeks or months. What Leavitt established was that the length of this cycle was related to what is called the star's luminosity—essentially, the amount of light it is emitting. This means that if you watch such a star go through its cycle, you can deduce how much light it is giving off. Then, by comparing this with the amount you actually receive, you can tell how far away it is.

The point is that with the resolving power of the Mount Wilson telescope, Hubble was able to pick out individual Cepheid variables in the nebulae, and therefore find out how far away they were. When the distances turned out to be millions of light years—much too far away to be in the Milky Way—Hubble established beyond doubt that the matter in the universe was organized into galaxies.

But his work didn't stop there. Other astronomers had noted that light from the nebulae was red shifted—that is, the light emitted (for example) by a hydrogen atom in a nebula had a longer wavelength than the same light emitted by a hydrogen atom in a terrestrial laboratory. This shifting is the result of the Doppler effect, and implies that the nebula is moving away from us—the bigger the shift, the faster the recession. Without a knowledge of the distances to the nebulae, however, no overall pattern could be deduced from these initial observations. A fast moving galaxy, for example, could be close to Earth or far away. There was no way of telling.

Armed with his new distance determinations, however, Hubble was able to show that there was a regular pattern in the data. The farther away a galaxy was, the faster it was moving away from us. This regularity, which has since been verified for millions of galaxies, is known as Hubble's Law and summarized in the equation

$$V = HD$$

where V is the velocity of the galaxy, D the distance to it, and H a number known as Hubble's constant.

Hubble's work established the fact that the universe is expanding. It is, however, a strange kind of expansion. It's not like pieces of an artillery shell moving outward from an explosion. The usual analogy used to help people picture the Hubble expansion involves the homely process of making a loaf of raisin bread. If you imagine standing on any raisin while the dough is rising, you will see the other raisins moving away from you because of the expansion of the dough. The farther away a raisin is, the faster it will be moving. No raisin is actually moving through the dough, however. They are carried away from each other by the expansion of the dough itself. In the same way, galaxies move away from each other because of the expansion of space itself, but do not move through space very much themselves.

This analogy explains one feature of the Hubble expansion that often puzzles students—the fact that the Earth seems to be the center of the Hubble expansion. If you think of the rising bread dough, however, you will realize that it makes no difference which raisin you stand on, you will always see yourself standing still and everything else moving away from you. In other words, everyone sees himself or herself as the center of the Hubble expansion—this is just a property of an expanding space-time grid.

You can also learn something important about cosmology by imagining a process by which we 'run the film backwards' for the Hubble expansion. All the matter in the universe would start to crunch together as we went backwards, heating up as it is compressed. As the compression proceeds, the collisions between particles would become more violent, first tearing the electrons from atoms, then breaking the nuclei down to elementary particles, then breaking the particles down to their fundamental constituents.

The study of the very early stages of the evolution of the universe has been one of the great scientific achievements of this generation. We have seen that to understand the largest thing we know about—the universe— we have to understand the smallest things—the quarks and (perhaps) the strings that constitute them. Today we can reproduce in our accelerator laboratories the conditions that existed when the universe was ten microseconds old, speak confidently (in terms of theory) about events that transpired when the universe was 10^{-35} seconds old, and speculate about the beginning itself.

At the same time that this theoretical work was going on, two unexpected observational results expanded our view of how the universe is put together.

DARK MATTER

In the 1970s, astronomer Vera Rubin of the Carnegie Institution of Washington was involved in mapping out what are called galactic rotation curves. These are graphs that show how fast objects like stars are moving as a function of their distance from the center of the galaxy. In general, we expect to see three different regimes in this sort of data. The first should be seen near the galactic center, where stars are close and tightly locked together. In this region the stars rotate like a wheel, with the speed increasing as we move away from the center (think of the stars as being on the platform of a merry-go-round). This phenomenon is called, appropriately enough, 'wheel flow'. Farther out, we should have a region where all the stars move at the same speed, regardless of their distance from the center. In this situation, the outer stars will slowly fall behind—it is this feature that gives galaxies their characteristic pinwheel appearance. Finally, when we are far enough away from the center for the main part of the galaxy to look like a small central mass, we should have a situation like that which obtains in the solar system, in which the outer planets move more slowly than the inner ones. This is called 'Kepler flow', after the astronomer who first worked out the systematics of the solar system. In effect, the onset of Kepler flow marks the point at which you leave the main mass of the galaxy and enter the sparsely populated outer regions.

When Rubin began her investigations, she found something both unexpected and exciting. It turned out that she couldn't see the onset of Kepler flow in any of the galaxies she observed no matter how far out she went, even if she was looking outside the starry region we usually think of as constituting the galaxy proper. The only way to explain this was to say that all of the visible part of the galaxy is encased in a sphere of material we can't see, but which exerts a gravitational influence and extends far beyond the collection of stars we normally think of as being the galaxy proper. Because this material neither absorbs nor emits electromagnetic radiation (we would see it if it did), it has been named 'dark matter'. It is estimated that 90 percent of the mass of a galaxy like the Milky Way is due to dark matter.

Since then, the presence of dark matter has been detected in many galaxies and in large clusters of stars, where it seems to act as a sort of gravitational glue holding the cluster together. The current consensus is that dark matter is some sort of elementary particle—either a familiar one in a new setting or one that hasn't as yet been directly detected in the laboratory. The generic name for these candidates is 'Weakly Interacting Massive Particles', or WIMPs.

DARK ENERGY

Another astonishing discovery was made in the 1990s, when astronomers uncovered yet another hitherto unknown component of the universe. To understand this discovery, think for a moment about the effect of gravity on the Hubble expansion. An outward-moving galaxy will feel the gravitational pull of other galaxies and, like a ball thrown upward in the Earth's gravitational field, it should slow down. The measurement of this deceleration would be one way of determining the total density of the universe—the bigger the deceleration, the greater the density. The deceleration would be seen most easily in very distant galaxies, whose light has been travelling to Earth for billions of years, because the difference between the expansion rates then and now would be the greatest. The problem is that these galaxies are so far away that even the best telescopes cannot pick out individual stars like Cepheid variables, so the technique that Hubble used to measure distance is not available. A new way of determining distance has to be found.

Enter the Type Ia supernova. These arise in double star systems where one of the partners has run through its life cycle and become a white dwarf—a star about the size of the Earth. As this star moves in orbit around its partner it pulls some of the partner's material (mostly hydrogen) off and gradually builds up a layer of hydrogen on its surface. This increase in mass raises the temperature of the star's core and eventually ignites a powerful thermonuclear reaction. The star literally explodes, emitting much of its energy as light, and for a while may even outshine the galaxy in which it is located.

The point is that for theoretical reasons, we know that all white dwarves have the same mass when this explosion occurs, which means that all Type Ia supernovae must have about the same luminosity (i.e. must give off about the same amount of light). Thus, as was the case with the Cepheid variables, if we know how much light we are receiving from a Type Ia supernova, we can deduce how far away it is. Because the supernovae are so bright, this then becomes a way of getting the distance to very remote galaxies and this, in turn, allows us to measure the rate of expansion of the universe billions of years ago.

There were some formidable technical obstacles that had to be overcome before these measurements could actually be made, but by the mid-1990s a stunned cosmological community learned that the Hubble expansion wasn't slowing down at all—it was speeding up. Something had to be acting as a kind of anti-gravity, pushing the galaxies apart and overcoming the inward pull of gravity. (It is probably more accurate to think of this effect as being due to a negative pressure rather than to 'antigravity'.) Astrophysicist Michael Turner of the University of Chicago coined the term 'dark energy' to describe the cause of the acceleration.

We have to stress that despite the apparent similarity in terminology, dark energy and dark matter are two completely different things. Dark matter is (presumably) a collection of massive particles (the WIMPs mentioned earlier) that exert an ordinary gravitational influence. Whatever dark energy is, it exerts a negative pressure that, on the large scale, has a repulsive (as opposed to attractive) effect.

Since the initial discovery of the accelerated expansion, detailed measurements have been made that allow us to trace out the history of the Hubble expansion. If you think of ordinary gravity as being a kind of brake on the expansion and dark energy as being kind of an accelerator or gas pedal, then for the first five billion years or so the brakes were on and the expansion actually slowed down. At about that time, however, the galaxies had gotten far enough apart to weaken the attractive effect of matter, and dark energy took over. The universe, in effect, stepped on the gas pedal and the expansion has been accelerating ever since.

Having said this, we have to say that at the present time no one has a clear idea of what dark energy is. Given that (as we shall see shortly) it makes up almost three-quarters of the mass of the universe, determining the nature of dark energy is probably the most important problem to be solved in the physical sciences, and perhaps the most important scientific question to be answered today in any area of science.

EINSTEIN'S GREATEST BLUNDER

When Einstein first wrote down the equations of general relativity, Hubble's work was still more than a decade in the future and the general consensus was that the universe was static, exhibiting no expansion or contraction. If matter was the only significant source of gravitation, such a universe would tend to collapse inward on itself. To avoid this outcome, Einstein somewhat arbitrarily added a term known as the cosmological constant (customarily denoted by the Greek letter capital lambda—Λ) to his equation. The function of this term was to prevent the collapse.

Once Hubble established the universal expansion, the cosmological constant was no longer needed and was dropped from the equations of general relativity. Einstein is often quoted as saying that introducing this term was 'the greatest blunder' of his life. There is some scholarly argument over whether he actually said this—this might be a situation like the one we encountered with Lord Kelvin in Chapter 2, where he is supposed to have said that the future of science was nothing more than a search for the next decimal place.

Whether he actually made this statement or not, the cosmological constant has made a comeback in recent years. At the present time it is the leading candidate to explain the nature of dark energy. This is because you can think of the cosmological constant as being the energy of the vacuum or, equivalently, regard it as a kind of cost for creating space-time. Unfortunately, when theorists try to put numbers into this idea, the results are wildly off. Whether this will change in the future is unknown.

An alternative theory goes by the name of 'quintessence'. It postulates the presence of a field that can vary in space and time, unlike the cosmological constant which never varies. The name harks back to Aristotle, who postulated the existence of the ether as a kind of 'fifth element' (in addition to earth, fire, air, and water). There is, at present, no evidence for this theory.

THE FATE OF THE UNIVERSE

The classical way of thinking about the fate of the universe is to ask how the Hubble expansion could evolve. The expansion could go on forever (a situation astronomers refer to as an 'open' universe) or it could reverse itself (a situation astronomers refer to as a 'closed' universe). The boundary between these futures, in which the expansion just coasts to a stop after an infinite amount of time, is called a 'flat' universe.

Which of these futures will actually come about depends on the amount of mass in the universe. The amount needed to produce a flat universe—what astronomers refer to as the amount needed to 'close' the universe—is customarily denoted by a capital Greek omega, Ω, and other masses are customarily described as fractions of Ω. Ordinary matter—the familiar stuff that makes up atoms and the rest of the familiar world, comprises only about 5 percent of the mass needed to close the universe. Throw in dark matter and you get about 27 percent more. The remainder of the mass of the universe is made up of dark energy. It is sobering that we don't know the identity of what turns out to be the main component of the universe.

Nevertheless, we can talk about what the fate of the universe could be for different possible forms of dark energy. For example, if dark energy is created by the expansion of the space-time grid, then the large-scale repulsion will get stronger and stronger as the expansion proceeds. Eventually it will start to tear galaxies, stars, and maybe even atoms apart—an outcome that astronomers have called the 'Big Rip'. If, on the other hand, the amount of dark energy is fixed and if, like gravity, its effects diminish with distance, the current acceleration might be a temporary phase in the life of the universe and gravity might step on the brakes again some time in the future. To know what awaits us in the far distant future, then, we're going to have to solve the riddle of dark energy.

We can close this discussion of the future by mentioning two reasonably certain events whose timing does not depend on dark energy. In about four billion years, our nearest large galactic neighbor, the Andromeda galaxy, will collide with the Milky Way. (This isn't a violation of Hubble's Law—the overall expansion does not preclude the presence of small local variations.) This may or may not have a major effect on the solar system, depending on the details of the motion of stars in the two galaxies.

Shortly thereafter, in about five and a half billion years, the sun will run out of hydrogen fuel in its core and go through its death throes. It will temporarily swell up, swallowing Mercury, Venus, and (possibly) the Earth. It will then shrink down to a white dwarf, a planet-sized object incapable of further nuclear reactions. Eventually it will radiate away its energy and become a dark cinder in the sky. In a sense, unless humans have managed to leave our home planet by that time, what happens later because of the effects of dark energy is somewhat academic.

14

THE FUTURE OF RELATIVITY

There was a door to which I found no key
There was a veil past which I could not see.

Rubaiyat of Omar Khayam

Relativity is a living science. As we have seen, it is intimately tied to modern cosmological theories, and is thus clearly a part of forefront scientific research. We have also seen that it has moved, as scientific advances usually do, from the research frontier to technology, with the prime example of this development being the Global Positioning System. Nevertheless, there are a number of outstanding questions whose resolutions will involve relativity in one way or another. One of these—the question of the nature of dark energy—was discussed in the last chapter. In what follows we will look at a few more of these issues, confining our attention to questions that might be resolved in the next few decades.

WILL RELATIVITY REMAIN ODD MAN OUT?

In Chapters 10 and 11 we pointed out that the explanation of the gravitation given by general relativity is fundamentally different from the explanation of the other three fundamental interactions given by quantum physics. This is a crucial point, because we know that if we apply general relativity to smaller and smaller objects, we will eventually get to the point where quantum effects will become important. This simple fact means that the dichotomy between gravity and the other interactions will have to be resolved, because it is the other interactions that govern the quantum world.

The attempt to put gravity on the same footing as the other interactions has a long history, beginning with Einstein's attempt to unify gravity and electromagnetism which we discussed in Chapter 1. In our time it has been addressed by some of the best minds in theoretical physics. Nonetheless, it remains an unsolved problem (some would say *the* unsolved problem) in physics today.

One approach to this problem, identified with cosmologist Steven Hawking, is to treat quantum effects as a kind of small perturbation on general relativity. This approach has led to a number of important results, such as the conclusion that over long periods of time black holes will evaporate and disappear because of a phenomenon known as Hawking radiation. (This is a process by which the energy in the gravitational field near a black hole is converted into a particle-antiparticle pair, one of which escapes and carries energy away.) This approach cannot be the final answer to the dichotomy problem, however, since it won't work when quantum effects get big.

Two of the leading contenders that put gravity on the same footing as the other forces are called string theory and loop quantum gravity. We'll discuss them separately below.

In a sense, we could say that string theory goes all the way back to Pythagoras, who investigated the vibrations of string in musical instruments. A plucked guitar string vibrates at many frequencies—the lowest frequency corresponding to the simplest up and down motion of the entire string, to which are added a series of overtones that involve more complex vibrations and give the instrument its richness of tone. The main idea of string theory is that the fundamental particles of matter correspond to different kinds of vibrations of strings. In this scheme, it is the strings themselves that are the fundamental constituents of matter.

From our point of view the most important result of string theory is that when the calculations are done, it turns out that one of the possible vibrations corresponds to a massless particle whose spin is twice that of the photon. This particle is the graviton, the particle whose exchange gives rise to gravitation. Other modes of vibration give rise to the other exchanged particles discussed in Chapter 10, so that in string theory gravity enters on the same footing as all the other fundamental interactions.

Having said this, we have to point out a couple of unusual aspects to strings—for one thing, they are very small, and for another they vibrate in a many-dimensional space. Current thinking is that the strings have a characteristic length of about 10^{-35} meters, a distance known as the Planck length. This is many orders of magnitude smaller than particles like the proton, whose characteristic size is typically around 10^{-15} meters. This means that we will probably never have accelerators with enough energy to 'see' the strings directly, so that any conclusions about the validity of the theory will have to be based on indirect tests.

There are many different versions of string theory, but physicists have been able to show that they are all equivalent to each other. In all of them, however, the only way to avoid certain types of unacceptable mathematical difficulties is to have the strings vibrating in multiple dimensions—10 or 26, depending on the version we're talking about. Since we live in four dimensions (three space and one time), this creates conceptual problems when we try to apply string theory to the real world. The usual way to get around this problem is to argue that the other dimensions are actually present, but are too small to be seen.

Here's an analogy that might help you understand this argument. Think about a garden hose. Seen from far away, the hose looks like a line. There is only one way to move along the hose—forward or backward—so that as far as we are concerned, the hose is a one-dimensional object. If we get closer, however, we see that the hose has width and height, which means that it has two more dimensions—dimensions we couldn't see from far away. In a similar way, string theorists argue, the extra dimensions in which strings vibrate aren't normally detectable to us but we would detect them if we could get down to the characteristic length of the strings themselves.

Instead of trying to bring gravity and the other interactions together by looking at the properties of particles, loop quantum gravity begins by looking at the properties of space and time. The end result of the complex theoretical mathematics is that when we get down to the Planck length, space and time are no longer smooth and continuous. Instead, they become granular or, to use the technical term, quantized. One way to visualize this is to imagine space and time as being made of a set of interlinked loops, sort of like chain mail, but with the fabric looking smooth and continuous when viewed from a distance. As with string theory, in loop quantum gravity, gravity emerges on an equal footing with the other fundamental interactions.

Loop quantum gravity requires a fundamental re-thinking of the nature of space and time, something analogous to Einstein's rethinking of these quantities in special relativity. In conventional physics, space and time form a continuous background against which events play out. In loop quantum gravity, space and time become players in the game in a new and complicated way. A common way of saying this is to note that in loop quantum gravity, the stage becomes an actor in the play.

Which (if either) of these two approaches to extending general relativity and bringing gravity into line with the other interactions will turn out to be right can't be predicted at this time. They do, however, mark the current frontier of our thinking about the fundamental nature of the universe.

GRAVITATIONAL WAVE DETECTORS

In Chapter 12 we discussed the prediction of the existence of gravitational waves and the indirect evidence for their existence that came from the study of pulsar rotation rates. In recent years scientists have started to look for direct evidence of the presence of these waves, and plans for some truly amazing experiments are on the drawing boards.

The main instrument now in operation is called LIGO (Laser Interferometer Gravitational Wave Observatory), with twin installations in Louisiana and Washington State. You can think of LIGO as an L-shaped vacuum chamber, with each arm of the L being about 4 kilometers long. The basic idea is that a beam of light from a laser is split at the crux of the L, with each split beam going down a different branch. At the end of each arm is a mass with a mirror attached. The laser beam bounces off the mirror and returns back to its starting point, where it recombines with the other beam.

In Chapter 12 we described the alternate compression and extension that gravitational waves produce when they encounter a massive object. You can think of the two ends of LIGO as being the edges of an object several kilometers across. It is expected that a gravitational wave passing through the detector will cause a change in the length of the arms of the

L on the order of 10^{-18} meters—about a thousandth of the distance across a proton. As incredible as it may seem, such accuracy can be attained in the apparatus. There are two detectors because this allows us to be able to rule out chance events masquerading as gravitational waves at just one detector site. A true gravitational wave would, of course, trigger both detectors. LIGO began taking data in 2002 and shut down for renovation in 2010. No gravitational wave events were seen. It reopened in 2014 with its sensitivity increased by a factor of 10.

The next generation of gravitational wave detectors may be in space, not on Earth. LISA (Laser Interferometer Space Antenna) started out as a joint venture between NASA and the European Space Agency (ESA). In 2011, however, NASA pulled out for financial reasons and ESA is developing the idea on its own though it too faces financial challenges. The apparatus would consist of three satellites at the points of an equilateral triangle—think of them as being the crux and arm ends of an L. The length of the arms would be about 100,000 kilometers and, if it is ever built, an apparatus like LISA would detect gravitational waves that have been bouncing around the universe since the Big Bang. Whether it will be built is probably more of a matter of politics than science at this stage.

THE MULTIVERSE

It is fitting that we close this book with a brief discussion of the concept of the multiverse. This concept arises from the attempt to bring together general relativity and quantum physics exemplified by string theory. In a sense, it is the final step on the road on which Albert Einstein embarked in the Swiss patent office so long ago. He didn't see it as a possibility, of course, but I think he would have been very much at home with it.

You can think of the multiverse as the ultimate outcome of the Copernican revolution. Copernicus taught us that the Earth is not the center of the universe and astronomers have shown that our sun is one star in a galaxy among billions in the universe. The multiverse suggests that our universe might be just one among many. Here's an analogy to help you visualize what this idea entails.

Imagine an undulating surface full of hills and valleys, and imagine rolling a ball over that surface. The ball will eventually settle into a valley—not necessarily the deepest valley, but in a valley somewhere. In string theory, these undulating hills represent a kind of energy, each of the valleys could correspond to a possible universe. The entire assemblage of hills and valleys is called the string theory 'landscape', and it is huge—it contains something like 10^{500} possible universes—a number that is, for all practical purposes, indistinguishable from infinity. This is what is called the 'multiverse'.

There are many versions of the multiverse, as there are many versions of string theory. The easiest one to visualize imagines each universe as being a kind of self-contained bubble. In some versions of the theory, for example, an expanding universe like ours is shedding little baby universes as it expands—a process that is going on even as you read these words.

The reason that the multiverse has attracted so much attention is that it provides a way of dealing with an old problem in cosmology—the so-called 'fine-tuning problem'. The problem can be stated in this way: if the fundamental constants of nature were different from what they are, life could not exist in our universe. For example, if the gravitational interaction were stronger, the Hubble expansion would have collapsed back in on itself before life could develop. If it were weaker, stars and planets would never have formed. If the strong and electromagnetic interactions were much different, nuclei and atoms wouldn't have formed. The biggest fine-tuning problem involves the cosmological constant (see Chapter 13), which is almost zero in our universe but which theory predicts should be much larger. It's no wonder that some theologians have advanced the fine tuning of the universe as proof for the existence of God.

Cosmologist Steven Hawking is one of the scientists who have enlisted the multiverse as a way of dealing with the fine-tuning problem. The argument goes like this: suppose that the fundamental constants of nature vary randomly from one universe to another in the multiverse. Then, just by chance, there will be some corner of the multiverse where the constants are just right for the development of life. The right way to ask the question, then, is not 'Why are the constants of nature fine tuned?' but 'Why are the constants of nature fine tuned, *given that an intelligent life form is asking the question?*' In most universes, the constants are wrong and the question never gets asked, but the fact that we are asking it means we are in one of those finely tuned universes.

It doesn't matter how many universes aren't finely tuned—we know that at least one is. It reminds me of what my old statistics prof used to call 'the golf ball on the fairway' problem. If, before you drive, you calculate the probability that the ball will land on a particular blade of grass, you will get an answer that is essentially zero. Yet the ball will land on one blade of grass somewhere, and it's no good asking why it landed there and not somewhere else. The point is that if it hadn't landed on that blade, it would have landed somewhere else equally improbable.

In the same way, it's no use asking why our universe has the unlikely collection of constants of nature that it has. If it didn't, then life would have developed in another, equally improbable universe and the same question would be asked there. Thus, the argument goes, the mere fact that we are here shows us that we've landed on a special 'blade of grass'—a finely tuned universe.

INDEX